Effective
Assessment
in the Early Years
Foundation Stage

Jan Dubiel

EX **Early Excellence**
Centre for Inspirational
Learning

Los Angeles | London | New Delhi
Singapore | Washington DC

SAGE Publications Ltd
1 Oliver's Yard
55 City Road
London EC1Y 1SP

SAGE Publications Inc.
2455 Teller Road
Thousand Oaks, California 91320

SAGE Publications India Pvt Ltd
B 1/I 1 Mohan Cooperative Industrial Area
Mathura Road
New Delhi 110 044

SAGE Publications Asia-Pacific Pte Ltd
3 Church Street
#10-04 Samsung Hub
Singapore 049483

First published © Jan Dubiel 2014

Library of Congress Control Number:
2013944802

British Library Cataloguing in Publication data

A catalogue record for this book is available from the British Library

ISBN 978-1-4462-7446-0
ISBN 978-1-4462-7447-7 (pbk)

Editor: Jude Bowen
Assistant editor: Miriam Davey
Project manager: Jeanette Graham
Production editor: Nicola Marshall
Copyeditor: Rosemary Campbell
Proofreader: Thea Watson
Indexer: Anne Solomito
Marketing manager: Catherine Slinn
Cover designer: Wendy Scott
Typeset by: Dorwyn, Wells, Somerset
Printed in Great Britain by Henry Ling Limited, at the Dorset Press, Dorchester, DT1 1HD

Contents

was to have a profound impact on my thinking about the relationship between assessment, pedagogy and effective outcomes for children. The impact of their work has been immense and they remain a constant and vibrant source of inspiration and expertise.

Jane Golightly was the Early Years Adviser for York, and demonstrated her faith in my unproven ability by appointing me as a Consultant and taught me through example how to work with the challenges and possibilities of strategic management; when in that role myself I would often secretly ask myself 'what would Jane do in this situation?'. The innovative 'Shared Foundation' that was established at the time had a strong influence on my thinking and understanding about the importance of continuity and the role that effective assessment plays in ensuring that the needs of 'unique learners' are met.

I am thankful to Pauline Hoare – most especially for her unofficial tutorials when I first joined the National Assessment Agency (NAA) and the discreet and clinical manner in which she inducted me into the murky and surreal world of national educational politics. Most importantly she taught me how to negotiate the seemingly treacle-filled pathways between the oblique political considerations and how to establish and support what is right for the successful development of young children.

I have also been incredibly fortunate to work with Brenda Spencer in various contexts over the past years; she was and is one of the most significant yet unsung influences on recent good Early Years policy developments. She remains a quiet yet towering and highly respected force in the Early Years community and I have benefitted massively from her on-going support, enthusiasm, determination and sheer intellect.

I am also grateful to my colleague Dr Lynne Edwards for her discussion and development of the concept and language around 'significances' and 'signifiers' of children's learning; and the other colleagues whom I had the privilege of working with during my time at NAA/QCDA, especially Becky Trafford, Rebecca Robinson, Sharon Keep, Tricia Carroll and Avril Mawle, with whom it was always a pleasure to share the challenges of our responsibilities.

Over the past years, Early Excellence has become both a national reference point for the development of effective Early Years practice and a source of principled vision for the Early Years community. It is no accident that the aforementioned colossi all have an on-going relationship with the organisation as trainers and conference speakers. I would additionally like to take this opportunity to personally thank Liz Marsden, the founder and director, for her support while writing this book.

One of the strongest influences on how we think about and regard children's learning emanates from the work of Professor Ferre Leavers, which is so vividly brought to life by Julia Moons. Through their increasingly close relationship with Early Excellence and the development of joint projects it has been an honour to work closely with him and observe the depth and intricacies of his approach and intellect at such close proximity.

Finally, I am deeply grateful to Matthew Sayer and Felicity Benton at Early Excellence for sourcing and organising the case studies and examples that have been used to illustrate the ideas in this book, and to the following practitioners and settings for taking the time and energy to provide them:

Leah Burke, Children's Place Day Nurseries, Bradford
Anne Webster, Holy Trinity C of E Primary School, Halifax
Jo Hager, Windhill Primary School, Doncaster
All the EYFS staff at Lark Hill Community Primary School, Salford

About the Author

Jan Dubiel is the National Development Manager at Early Excellence and works as part of the team to support Early Years practitioners and settings in all aspects of practice and provision. Having trained as an Early Years specialist, Jan worked as a Nursery, Reception and Year 1 teacher in schools across the country, leading teams as an Early Years Co-ordinator. Following roles as an Early Years Consultant and Senior Adviser, he was appointed by the then Qualifications and Curriculum Authority (QCA) to lead on the management of the (Early Years) Foundation Stage Profile and had national responsibility for its implementation and moderation, developing guidance and support materials and working at a strategic level with policy makers. Jan has developed a national and international reputation as a conference speaker, consultant and trainer and he has written widely on different aspects of Early Years pedagogy.

1

Introduction – Reclaiming Assessment

This chapter will:

- Explore the nature and existing definitions of the term 'assessment'
- Identify and challenge mythologies associated with assessment
- Establish a balanced and accurate definition of assessment in Early Years pedagogical theory and practice
- Explore the notion of 'significance' and 'signifiers' in children's learning and development
- Clarify key terminology

When we work with children we connect ourselves to the future – through the inspiration, guidance and wisdom that we provide, and through the influence and impact we have on children's lives, their understanding and their perceptions of themselves and the world around them. Although this is a future that we may not necessarily see, it is one that we help to shape and one that we are ultimately responsible for (Postman 1982). After all, today's children are tomorrow's citizens, its leaders, thinkers, policy makers, innovators and entrepreneurs (Katz 2008). The world we will live in many years from now will be the one governed, organised and enriched by the children we have worked with.

This impact, and by association its responsibility, is even more significant when working with children aged birth to 5. Studies such as Wikart/Perry Preschool study (Schweinhart et al. 2005) and the on-going Effective Pre-School and Primary Education (EPPE) study (Sylva et al. 2010) demonstrate the critical influence that pre-school provision can have on outcomes and life chances for children well into their adulthood. Equally significant is the growing evidence (Sylva et al. 2012) that the *quality* of such provision is one of the most powerful and influential variables, and that the outcomes for children – in all aspects of life – can be strongly determined by this. When this is coupled with neurological evidence that identifies this age range as the most significant in the growth and development of the brain (Shore 1997; Whitebread 2012) then the responsibility becomes an even more stark and weighty one. By the time children start formal schooling much of their sense of themselves is already formed, their understanding of the world around them starting to take definite shape. Neurologically, it is believed that up to 85% of their lifetime dendritical and synaptic connections – the physical basis on which learning is created – have already taken place. Far from the traditionalist view that school is the point at which learning starts, what happens then builds directly on what has already taken place (Shore 1997).

The role of the practitioner in every Early Years setting is by its nature a multi-faceted one (Rose and Rogers 2012). Multiple decisions are taken on a second-by-second basis to ensure that the most effective and life enriching opportunities are available to children and that their learning and development continues to be supported, facilitated and extended. Conscious as practitioners are of the dramatic responsibility they bear, there is a continual awareness of the need to optimise each moment to most effectively enable and empower children as thinkers and learners. Learning is a constant process; neurological connections are continually being formed, adopted, reconfigured and pruned; the brain continually reshapes and 'sculpts' its knowledge, understanding and 'cognitive flexibility'. The practitioner's role is to shape and guide this learning so that it is useful, meaningful and applicable to the lives of the children they work with, knowing that birth to 5, the period covered by the terminology of 'Early Years', is the most rapidly intense and important period of growth.

Working mostly through their 'informed intuition', their experiences, wealths of expertise, knowledge and their highly refined, complex skills in translating and converting these into action, practitioners continually adapt their responses, ask questions, make assertions and provide challenge and support to the children they work with. This is how the fragmented tesserae of each interaction, each conversation, each suggestion, provocation and moment of direct teaching culminate in the skilful, well-equipped, inquisitive, confident and creative children that we, as practitioners, proudly usher into the next phase of their learning.

A key aspect of this process and a critical facet of the practitioner's role is that of assessment.

The purpose of this book is to focus specifically on this aspect by defining and exploring the critical role and purpose of assessment in effective Early Years pedagogy, examining the considerations and challenges that practitioners face in their day-to-day practice. It will combine an analysis of the theoretical and philosophical aspects required to understand it with a practical overview of how this might translate itself into considerations for everyday practice. Finally, it will link directly to the current statutory assessment requirements through the English Early Years Foundation Stage framework and the specifics of the 'Two Year Old Progress Check' and the EYFS Profile.

This book has been written for practitioners, headteachers, managers, trainers, policy makers and all those with an interest in ensuring that the experiences and opportunities that children have in the Early Years are the most meaningful and effective that they can be. Throughout the book I use the term 'successful' as the key aspiration and outcome for children. It is important to note that this refers to a broad definition of success that may include, but is not exclusively, what might be defined as 'academic'. Success in the sense that I use it refers to a broad and deep skill and knowledge set that could be referred to as 'life skills', and which incorporates aspects of cognitive, creative, emotional, social and personal as well as purely academic notions of success.

Mythologies and misunderstandings

Of all the areas of Early Years practice, it appears that it is the approach to and understanding of assessment that remains the most confused, maligned, misunderstood and misused (Tickell 2011). It is subject to the most extreme and resilient mythology – however ludicrous – and still often appears to operate on the basis of a 'folk-lore' model (Carr 2001) that serves the purpose of expedience and convenience rather than increasing our information base of how children demonstrate their significant knowledge and under-standing. This tension is a critical one to resolve, as an effective and sensible approach to assessment is fundamental to meaningful and inclusive practice. It is also crucial to be aware of, and challenge head on, the dangers of over-complicating what is a critical yet intuitive (and sometimes counter-intuitive/'informed' intuition) aspect of successful and effective Early Years pedagogy and practice.

So the title of this chapter – 'Reclaiming Assessment' – is a deliberately and consciously provocative one, as it seeks to redefine and reconceptualise what the term means and how we perceive it, and this is ultimately what will impact most strongly on practice and provision in Early Years settings. Above all, effective assessment operates as the most potent lever for self-reflection, change and development of practice (Carr 2001). The understanding of assessment, its perception, and even the use of the word itself is subject to such wilful misunderstanding and misuse that practitioners can be forgiven for succumbing to its all-pervasive negativity and its multitude of nefarious, unwieldy and unnecessary baggage.

The following examples are all taken directly from my own experiences as a Local Authority Consultant and Adviser.

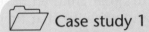

Case study 1

A well-resourced Travel Agents Role Play has been set up in the classroom following a visit to a local branch with the theme 'Journeys'. The children use the area very effectively, taking on the roles of Travel Agent and customer with enthusiasm and authenticity. One child ushers a potential client into the office to discuss the kind of holiday that they would like. 'Where would you like to visit?' she asks, 'How would you like to travel there?', 'What food would you like to eat when you are there?' and so on. On a clipboard she begins to record this information, spelling common words accurately and making phonetically plausible attempts at others such as 'afrika' and 'chps'. She is very skilled at the role, very involved in the activity and keen to complete the transaction. In the middle of this, the teacher calls her over to the table where she is 'assessing phonic knowledge'. The child is faced with a drawn picture of an apple tree containing a number of apples. Each apple has a single letter on. The teacher points to each of them and asks her what sound the letter makes. The child, anxious that the customer does not leave, completes this assessment activity as quickly as possible, continually turning round to make sure that the customer remains. When she is finally released to return she has only identified three of the letter sounds correctly.

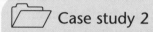 Case study 2

Whilst we are discussing the development of children in the setting, the practitioner wearily reaches up to a shelf and takes down a large and generously stuffed A3 folder from a number of similar ones alongside it. Inside, a detailed 'Learning Portfolio' itemises the child's achievements through a plethora of notes and photographs. Much of the information is similar and simple. 'Charlie made a tower out of bricks', 'Charlie completed a jigsaw', 'Charlie likes being outside' and so on. During the ensuing discussion the practitioner states that she spends much of her evenings updating the Portfolio for each child with information and photographs from the day. She declares it to be the most time-consuming task, and whenever anything happens in the setting her first thought is – 'how can I record that for the Portfolio?' When I ask her what happens to all this carefully stored information, she replies that sometimes parents might take it home at the end of the year, but she never looks at the Portfolio once the information has been added. 'Does the next practitioner or setting look a it?' I ask and she laughs; 'No, they wouldn't have time to wade through all this information for every single child'.

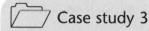 Case study 3

A practitioner has devised a complex grid, one for each child that lists specific statements of development grouped into self-created developmental bands. The separate statements within these bands are highlighted in different colours to indicate the time of year that they were 'achieved' by the child. On an attached document the outcomes from these are summarised into 'scores of attainment' that relate to each group of statements; each highlighted sentence counting as 1 'point'. Calculations have been made in order ascertain the 'progress' children are making within a term and across the year. I am told that they need to 'move up from one band to another every three months' and that there is an average score that the group should 'achieve' at the end of every half term.

Each of these separate examples demonstrates different aspects of the overwhelming mythology and misunderstanding of the process and purpose, and even meaning, of the concept of 'assessment'; what it is, what it is for, why and how we need to do it and the purpose of the information that it generates.

The perception, widely held, is often that assessment is a stand-alone, detached activity, required in order to complete formats and records, used for monitoring and calculating children's 'measurable progress', clinically judging and quantifying children in inappropriate ways that ultimately serve the convenience of a formula for numerical data and statisticians rather than the children themselves. Nor does it appear that this information is derived from what practitioners know about children from their day-to-day contact, conversations and observations. When policy, pedagogical and strategic decisions are taken as a result of this, then the information becomes disproportionately important, consequential and influential. If this then becomes the basis of the requirement for accountability, the separation from everyday practice and knowledge becomes a distinct and accepted 'lacuna' between the integrity and accuracy of information and its form and status.

It is also often assumed that the process of assessment is synonymous with the manufacture of vast and copious records – post-its, photographs and detailed written observations that provide tangible 'evidence' for the judgements and assertions that practitioners then make about children's learning and development. This process – record keeping and documentation – is terminology often used interchangeably with the term 'assessment'; in fact it is imperative that practitioners are aware that these are fundamentally different, as we shall explore later.

Additionally, in many quarters and schools of thought, assessment is viewed as the 'testing' of children, requiring them to perform to an adult-defined task, to 'pass' or 'fail' at this task or activity and then be subject to assumptions about their 'ability' and even 'intelligence' and potential as a result. For example, in one commercially available system, children are presented with a picture and asked to identify objects such as specific musical instruments or named water-based crafts. Their capability to be able to do or not do this contributes to a weighted score that then predicts the expectation for later attainment.

This deficit model that focuses on what children 'cannot do' or 'do not know' becomes the main driver, and when this is then linked to a set of 'targets' or expectations – however benignly intended – then the diverse nature and reality of children's development becomes lost in a sea of faceless numbers, charts and percentages that discard the reality of children as learners. Children are very astute and skilled in tuning in to what is important and soon pick up on the messages that these 'assessments' carry. There is much evidence to show how an early sense of failure can impact on a child's self-esteem and self-perception as a learner (Nutbrown and Carter 2012). (Dweck 2006) identifies the concept of 'mindset' as instrumental in success and achievement and argues that this is strongly affected by the perception that the learner develops of their own ability and potential. There is an understandable reaction to this type of 'testing' approach when the focus for such an activity is very young children for whom the spectrum of what would be considered typical development is enormous, and the resulting assumptions – erroneously arrived at – can have such lasting consequences.

It is hardly then a surprise that even the word 'assessment' itself has been imbued with a negative connotation that reflects all of these things and appears in a consistently pejorative way in blogs, discussion forums and the letters pages of periodicals. There is often, amongst practitioners, an adverse reaction to the word itself and it is held responsible for detracting from the specifics of everyday practice and compromising and diverting activity away from supporting children.

Therefore, there exists a profound and widespread misunderstanding of what assessment actually is, what processes it entails and what its purpose is.

Given this misunderstanding, and perception of assessment, it is perhaps important to define it in calm, measured and professional way that enables us to understand its nature, process and purpose fully.

Defining assessment

The definition by Vicky Hutchin (1996: 7), 'The purpose of the assessment process is to make explicit children's achievements, celebrate their achievements with them, then help them to move forward to the next goal', outlines clearly that as a starting point, the nature of assessment is a process rather than an single event. This is a considerable distance away from one of the anecdotal examples described previously, where children are removed from the activities they are involved in to an abstract unrelated task where they are then asked a set of questions. The clear implication of Hutchin's definition is that assessment is inextricably woven into day-to-day practice. It is a process that exists and sustains itself alongside, not in opposition to, children's activity. The process, as explored later and throughout this book, is a complex one that involves a different set of dynamics and strategies that inform and are informed by the decisions that practitioners take.

Equally pertinent is the phrase 'making explicit their achievements', as this is the focal point of acknowledging children's current stage of development, understanding and knowledge. We have long recognised the diversity of children's development and its unpredictability and idiosyncrasy, as well as the different, unique and sometimes baffling yet exciting trajectories that children's learning takes and the outcomes and expressions that form as a result. Children's perceptions of the world and how they fuse their emerging understanding is, if nothing else, magically unpredictable and often contrary and counter to experienced adult assumptions. It could be argued that as children are 'unfettered by knowledge' their perceptions and conclusions will often be unique. Fundamental to being able to sustain and develop this, facilitating appropriate support and challenge, is the practitioner's robust and skilful understanding of 'where the child is' and what is significant and relevant to that point in time and development. The use of the word 'achievement' rather than 'attainment' is highly significant here as this centres the practitioner's assessment activity and response on the individual needs and nature of the child. The existence of externally derived expectations, goals or targets is not relevant in this context as this focuses on the practitioner's wider and more important responsibility to the development and support for the individual child, at an individual point with an individual potential trajectory that the practitioner can see opening up in front of them. Critically too, the definition identifies the purpose; moving the child, wherever they are on their own individual learning and development spectrum, on to the next stage, the next possibility, the next skill, knowledge or understanding that will empower and extend them as a learner.

Assessment has no intrinsic value; it cannot exist meaningfully as a self-standing detached entity. The process of assessment is only as useful as the purpose for which it is used, the ways in which it is used, and the effect it has on how practitioners reflect on their pedagogy and the unique learning path that individual children take. In the hectic mêlée of Early Years practice, time and prioritising actions become a critical aspect of effectiveness. Therefore, practitioners need to consider very carefully how they ascribe time to make – and especially record – judgements about children's learning, and need to carefully consider the purpose of this, especially if this is not an integral part of their planning and development.

Mary Jane Drummond (1993) also provides us with a definition of assessment that poses three questions:

- What is there to see?
- How best can we understand what we see?
- How can we put our understanding to good use?

Again, the starting points are the reality of children, the nature of practitioner responsibility and an acknowledgement of what they bring as individuals through experiences to that moment in time. Similar approaches are also explored by Fisher (2008), Nutbrown (2001) and Carr (2001). The principle factor being that the starting point for assessment is not where we or anyone else thinks children should be but where they are, what they know and how they understand it. Drummond's questions assert that practitioners take that initial information as it is, process it through their knowledge, expertise and specialism and then utilise it to enhance and support those critically identified next steps of development and progression; what will later be explored as 'signifiers' and 'significances'.

Assessment could be further defined as 'the knowing and understanding of children' and it is a 'pedagogical behaviour' in that it is a constant feature of all our interactions with children, our thinking about them as learners and the actions we take as a result. It weaves its way through all aspects of professional and intuitive activity and cognition, influencing practitioners' thinking and actions on a multitude of levels that the 'multi faceted' role requires. During a typical day, Early Years practitioners take a multitude of continual decisions about how to act, to support, intervene and challenge children. The process of assessment, as an intrinsically pedagogical behaviour, critically provides the rationale for how this subsequently unfolds.

It has long been noted that the process exists, or should exist, comfortably alongside what practitioners already do (Kelly 1992). Throughout the day practitioners continually process the miasma of information that they are bombarded with, filtering out and differentiating between the significant, the routine, the known and the new. Every interaction, every conversation, every 'noticed behaviour' percolates into their knowledge and understanding of who children are, what they know and can do and what they need next in order to continue progressing and developing.

Central to this activity is the question; 'What do I know about this child?' – and this is the question to which the process of assessment provides the answer. Defined simply, assessment is practitioners knowing the children they work with, understanding their learning and being able to link this with the next steps in progression and development. Assessment is the dynamic process of translating 'what there is to see' into skilfully considered adult activity and support to enhance experiences and extend learning, thinking and knowing; 'putting the understanding to good use'. Within that, practitioners take additional decisions about what is appropriate, what is possible and what is meaningful for the child; effective pedagogy leads them to take account of interests, propensities, preferences and securities. Practitioners take all this information and carefully shape a response or a provocation or a 'teachable moment'. As adults, we enter the child's world, knowing what possibilities are there, possibilities that might be invisible to the child, but visible to the adult, as experience enables us to draw upon our wider and deeper knowledge of the world. These 'invisible moments of possibility' are formed from the knowledge we gain from 'assessing' children, finding out and translating the information that makes them who they are at that moment in time. Assessment, far from being a stand-alone, clinical, formulaic measurement, is a living, breathing dynamic, a facet of how we teach and empower learners. Within this we need to demonstrate the critical skills of 'tuning in' to that idiosyncratic development, seeing the possibility it presents and taking the decision on how best – if at all – to challenge and extend it. Particularly with experience, much of this happens on an intuitive level; often as an almost subconscious response to particular behaviour or actions.

Because of the nature of assessment, as with any behaviour that relies on intuition to such a great extent and is often subconscious in its delivery, practitioners will always need to be aware that it will invariably be a subjective exercise and that the decisions they take, specifically the assessments, will be as a result of the values they hold as educators and what they consider to be important, relevant, interesting, useful or significant. We choose to see what is important, what we value and what is significant to *us* as the viewer.

Fundamentally, assessment is an overt yet implicit statement of values. Pamela Moss notes that 'what isn't assessed tends to disappear from the curriculum' (quoted in Carr 2001: 180), and there is an irrefutable logic behind this. We assess, we notice – and we especially record – what we consider to be important. Conversely, if it isn't important enough to be assessed, to be noted, commented upon or processed cognitively in any way, then by definition there is no point in providing for it or teaching and facilitating it. So every time a practitioner makes a judgement a range of critical decisions have already been made. These, often implicitly rather than explicitly apparent, are the values and beliefs on which the practitioner bases their practice, provision and pedagogy. The origins of this will vary from practitioner to practitioner and will be wholly subject to culture, setting ethos, personal experience, training, and even what is perceived to be expected of them. Everything viewed, heard or even assumed, falls through this 'prism of values' and is then considered whether or not it is important enough to be realised.

Assessment is never an objective activity, nor can it ever be value free.

This has implications for the process, and defines key considerations for practitioners undertaking assessments.

Evidently 'what' we choose to assess will be greatly influenced by this, and the content of provision – what might be termed as the 'curriculum', or the body of information and skills that we think children will need in order to be successful – will be defined by and define what become the foci of assessment. In narrow, inappropriately focused curricula, the assessments that derive from it focus on the specifics of what is considered most important and relevant. Equally, the nature of 'learning behaviours' – how children react and apply their knowledges, skills and understandings, the traits and propensities which define them as individuals and the nature of their learning – also become pertinent.

Equally important is the 'how' we assess and the messages this gives to children about what we consider to be important in terms of the process of their learning and what we value. As previously stated, this impacts directly on children's understandings and how they process the clear and explicit messages from adults into their own definitions and understandings of what is important. The child in the Travel Agents was clearly aware that the practitioner valued mainly what was done in response to her questions, and although she did not commit to this as her involvement was in something far more interesting and significant, she fully accepted the 'summoning' by the practitioner as an important aspect of the relationship between them. Not only did this undermine the value of self-initiated activity and the wealth of information that it produces – clearly evident in the small vignette quoted previously – it ultimately provided inaccurate and misleading information. The child obviously had a good grasp of the phonetic code and was applying it skilfully in her play. This was not apparent in the adult-led 'test type assessment' that so pointlessly interrupted it.

So assessment relies heavily on the notion of 'significance' as this determines critical aspects of both the content and the process. It is worth being clear that this notion is a dual one and we might do well to adopt a 'split screen' (Claxton et al. 2011, quoted in Carr and Lee 2012) approach when considering it.

Different kinds of 'significance'

The significance for the child is based on new or confirmed behaviour and activity; something achieved for the first time or a consolidation of an understanding or mastery that was tentative though not yet secure. As practitioners who know the children they work with very well recognise, these can present themselves sometimes predictably in response, sometimes during unexpected moments of the day, and they 'log', notice or filter this because it carries a particular significance for that child. Evidently this will be different for different children and only through the day-to-day knowledge, built up from the intense relationship between the child and adult, will this information be apparent and obvious.

The other side to this significance concerns the practitioner; their values, beliefs and their own perceptions of what is considered to be important. In addition to what is significant for the child, practitioners will also consider what is significant for their on-going learning and the steps, support and encouragement needed to continue facilitating their development. As adults, indeed as a community or society, we decide what children need to be successful, and the skills and knowledges required to be able to participate and contribute. This is often why the content of curricula, and their associated assessments, are so keenly fought, as they define what society needs and values; the 'bodies of knowledge' we consider important enough to pass on to successive generations. During assessment we activate this significance as we steer and guide children towards the acquisition of the knowledge, skills and understanding we have decided – or have been told – are important and necessary. In current terminology this might refer to the specific, 'Curriculum Outcomes' 'Domains of Learning' or 'Areas of Learning and Development' that describe precisely the nature and content of such bodies of knowledge and set them in an important context and means by which learning and development can occur.

Therefore, with all this in mind, I would like to introduce the concept of 'signifiers' of learning to encompass and describe this dualistic, 'split screen' view of what children demonstrate and what we assess. A 'signifier' is a specific demonstration of a knowledge, skill or understanding that is significant either in terms of the child's individual development or the wider expectations of learning.

Assessment then, is the gathering of information, the translation of children's thought and activity into (generally adult-defined) signifiers of learning. However, implicit in all of this, though often subject particularly to externally driven pressures, is the absolute necessity of such information being authentic and accurate. Assessment information has no use; it cannot 'be put to good use' (Drummond 1993) if it is not accurate, authentic, real and honest. If the practitioner's judgements become influenced by 'what should be' or an external target or expectation, then its accuracy and integrity becomes severely compromised. It then becomes irrelevant to any use that could be made of it. Moreover, the biggest single negative impact of an inaccurate assessment will be on the child themselves. If a child is judged to be achieving or attaining at a higher level or stage of development than they actually are, then the next practitioner will set challenges and have expectations for that child that are unlikely to be met. The negative impact of this on the child themselves as a learner can sometimes be devastating. Conversely, if a child is assessed but is judged to be under the level or phase of development than is actually the case then challenges and expectations will be reduced accordingly and the child's opportunity to flourish and develop will be adversely affected.

The terminology of assessment

To conclude this introductory chapter, it is important to clarify through brief overviews the terminology regarding assessment processes and uses. Much of what has been written so far has illuminated the importance of perception and definition and of challenging the mythology, folklore and assumption around the process of assessment. This is even more apparent and important around the area of language and the terminology used. More than anything else, practitioners need to be clear about their own definitions and take ownership of recognised terms, in order to support their own beliefs and values and to enable them to impact effectively on their own interpretations of effective Early Years pedagogy.

Achievement is a development in understanding, skill or knowledge demonstrated by a child in relation to their own starting point. It is a fundamental principle of effective Early Years practice that children develop and achieve at a diverse range of rates and speeds. Because this is related to the individuality of the child themselves, wherever they may be on the learning and development spectrum, it is the most important aspect of the practitioner's role. The 'tuning in' to children's learning, and answering Drummond's question of 'what is there to see?', is wholly driven by the notion of individual achievement, as this will vary considerably from child to child.

Attainment refers to a fixed level of knowledge, skill or understanding. Attainment relates to a set of predetermined criteria which a child either is or is not able to demonstrate. Many approaches to assessment have attainment criteria at their core in order to make quantitative judgements about numbers of children attaining in specific areas; and much of the 'clinical' approach to assessment relies on this. Attainment does have a role in Early Years assessment but it must always be acknowledged that high attainment can still indicate low achievement and vice versa. Attainment is not always an effective indicator of progress or effective pedagogy.

Formative assessment is sometimes termed 'assessment for learning' and is the primary function of the assessment process. The translation of children's thinking and activity 'forms' the practitioner's view and understanding of their development, and this in turn enables them to take appropriate and measured decisions about how best to continue supporting and developing the child's learning and thinking. The necessity of formative assessment enables the practitioner to develop a clear and authentic view of children's learning and a real understanding of their current level of development and the next step in their learning (Fisher 2008).

Summative assessment is the summary of achievement and/or attainment and is characterised by defining a specific point in time when either achievements and/or attainments culminate. Summative assessments are derived from the on-going assessment process and feed necessarily into the process of formative assessment. Although the distinction between formative and summative assessment is a necessary one, it is not always helpful to differentiate between them; all assessments need to be formative in nature, with the summative aspect a 'momentary imprint' of the information.

A 'signifier' of learning, or a 'significance', is an action, demonstrated thought, concept, understanding or skill that is considered significant for the individual child's achievement or the wider developmental expectation or possibility. It might also refer to the mastery or understanding of a particular aspect of a defined curriculum.

Evidence is the information that a practitioner accesses to clarify an assessment; either formative or summative. This is the knowledge that the practitioner has, through various streams, in order to be secure and confident about an assertion or judgement for the child. The majority of evidence will derive from the daily on-going interaction and will be part of the practitioner's perception and understanding of the child as an individual learner. It is important that practitioners do not confuse the notion of evidence with records and documentation. It is quite possible to have evidence of what is known about a child without the need for it to be tangibly recorded.

Recording and documenting is the process of creating tangible archives and examples of children's attainment and achievements as the result of assessments undertaken by practitioners. There is frequent debate and misunderstanding about the purpose of this, its necessity and its role in the wider assessment process itself. The challenges and issues around records and documents often pertain to the notion of evidence and accountability, though it is also important that practitioners do not confuse assessment – looking at the on-going pedagogical behaviour – with records and documentation – the tangible manifestation of aspects of this. Practitioners, as professionals who know and understand the children they work with, will take individual decisions about the role, necessity and types of records they keep. It is also important to state that records serve assessment – 'the knowing and understanding of children' – and cannot act as a substitute for it.

Accountability is the means by which practitioners and settings justify and demonstrate the impact that their practice, provision and pedagogy have on the children they work with. While practitioners will be 'internally accountable' through their knowledge and expertise, they are often faced with a measure of 'external accountability' that can sometimes undermine and compromise this.

Progress is the journey children take towards greater mastery, knowledge and understanding (Bredekamp and Copple 1997). All children acquire additional skills and knowledge, become more proficient, develop expertise and refine and enhance themselves as learners. It is contestable whether or not this is 'measureable' in any authentic and realistic way or whether the 'signifiers' and significances of children's learning lend themselves to easy representation. Although it is quite possible and reasonable to describe and articulate the 'progress' that all children make, this should not be compromised by applying a simplistic formula for ease of expression.

Outcomes are the aspirations we have for children and the 'known world' that we induct children into. They are value driven and culturally defined. All educational philosophies have outcomes at their core whether or not these are explicitly defined. The notions of 'progress' and 'accountability' generally rest on the defined or implicit outcomes that practitioners and settings have for children.

Data is information that can be described in any way. This is not to be confused with 'numerical data' which is a specifically numerical expression of information.

Reflective task

Explore your own beliefs and understanding of the word 'assessment'. Where do they originate from? What are the contexts that you most use it in?

Further reading

Carr, M. (2001) *Assessment in Early Childhood Settings*. London: Paul Chapman.
Drummond, M.J. (1993) *Learning to See: Assessment through Observation*. York, ME: Stenhouse.
Glazzard, J., Chadwick, D., Webster, A. and Percival, J. (2010) *Assessment for Learning in the Early Years Foundation Stage*. London: SAGE.

2

Why is Assessment Important?

This chapter will:

- Explore the key considerations for understanding the importance of assessment within Early Years pedagogy
- Distinguish between and clarify the relative roles of content and process in making assessments
- Examine the relationship between assessment and values

In the previous chapter we explored the nature and definition of assessment and attempted to deconstruct its nature or 'essence' and to calmly separate it from the 'mythologies' and misconceptions that surround it. Clarity of definition, and understanding the reality, are important starting points. Different types and models of assessment were also discussed and the central, primary importance of 'assessment *for learning*' (Clarke 2001; Nutbrown and Carter 2012) as a means by which to support and enrich the lives of children was contrasted with other 'secondary' uses, that whilst having importance and purpose, should not override this primary central and important function. The notion of 'checks and balances' (Nutbrown and Carter 2012) or clinical 'measurements', though traditionally a common assumption about the purpose of assessment, need to be placed in the correct perspective. Essentially, these are the 'by-products' of the approach, content and perception of assessments undertaken; they are not determinants nor the real outcome or purpose.

Similarly, the existence and practice of formal/adult-directed/non-observational assessment, and particularly the use of 'tests' for young children was explored. There is general agreement amongst specialists and experts in the Early Years community that this is a singularly ineffective means of establishing an authentic and accurate view of 'signifiers' and significances in children's learning and development.

Key considerations for the importance of assessment

Drummond's (1993) three questions (see pages 8–9) refer in the first instance to that which practitioners use as dynamic everyday information; what is defined as 'formative assessment' that literally provides the information that forms and shapes next steps in learning, interactions, support and challenge. The conclusion, therefore, that assessment is 'the knowing and understanding of children in order to support their on-going learning and development' is a suitable place to re-start.

Carr (2001) calls this the 'business of educators' and argues that as part of this process we 'reframe the purpose, the outcomes, the items for intervention, the definitions of validity and progress, the procedures and the value for practitioners' (2001: 20). She goes on to identify two key questions that form the basis of her discussion:

1) How can we describe early childhood outcomes in ways that make valuable statements about learning and progress?

2) How can we assess early childhood outcomes in ways that promote and protect learning? (2001: 20)

Her exploration of the answers to these questions, in the form of the internationally renowned and highly influential 'Learning Stories' has assumed a position and status within Early Years practice and philosophy as a vibrant, practical and reflective expression of values and understanding of children as learners.

However, it is important to reflect on why it is that the approach and process of assessment generates such importance and impact, and why it retains and emanates such overwhelming power as a dimension of education and pedagogy. Why is it, as Broadfoot (1996) notes, that assessment is 'the most powerful policy tool' and a 'powerful source of *leverage* to bring about change'?

One of the starting points to consider this understanding could lie within Carr's (2001) approach and her exploration of the effective use of Learning Stories in New Zealand kindergartens and early childhood centres. In the text prior to the two questions previously cited, her assertion that 'Early childhood practitioners ... have to make some assumptions about learning ... that are informed and reflective' (2001: 20) is critical to understanding the importance of the role that assessment plays and why such heated and robust discussion continually surrounds it. It also illuminates the importance of approaches that are accurate, authentic, informed and principled.

Drummond (2008) makes the link between values and assessment explicit through the case study of an individual child whose success within some assessment models would have been severely limited yet who displayed high levels of achievement and intelligence; she prefaces this with her assertion that '... in the effective practice of assessment, educators make principled and *value-driven choices* about children, about learning and achievements. As a result they are able to make well-judged choices about the methods, purposes and outcomes of assessment' (2008: 3, my emphasis).

In another influential text, Shirley Clarke (2001) also champions the importance of formative assessment as the key purpose of the process:

> If we think of our children as plants, summative assessment of the plants is the process of simply measuring them. The measurements might be interesting to compare and analyse but in themselves they do not affect the growth of the plants. Formative assessment, on the other hand, is the garden equivalent of feeding and watering the plants – directly affecting their growth. (2001: 2)

Although this analogy is a useful and important one, in my view there needs to be a further layer – beneath the soil if you will – that underpins the understanding of the statement. *What* we feed and water the plants with, and *how* we feed them has a direct bearing on the outcomes, in this case the successful growth of the plants. As gardeners, we take decisions on what the plants need, how much water, fertiliser, sunlight and so on. All of these decisions come from our knowledge and beliefs and our intentions or aspirations for the plants – how we want the plants to grow and thrive successfully. So the act itself is far from being neutral. Millennia of horticulture have provided us with the knowledge of how to increase the likelihood of being successful at this and we continually reinvigorate and extend this knowledge as new scientific discoveries are made. Additionally, as gardeners, we make decisions about which plants are going to be most successful and dependant on the specific care, nurture and techniques we use.

The analogy with assessing children is an obvious one. The decisions we take about what and how we assess, what we choose to notice, value and even see are not neutral nor accidental. Our perceptions of children's learning in terms of both 'what' and 'how' come from deeply rooted values that are then informed by our own knowledge, experience and development as professionals. In the last chapter I discussed the definition(s) of 'signifiers' and 'significances', and how part of this rests with our decisions as adults and practitioners.

The role of content

Perhaps the most evident dimension of this is the 'content', the knowledges, skills and understandings that inform the assessments and the resulting judgements we make. Whether deliberate or not, assessment defines the outcomes and content of what children learn. However unintentional it may be, there is an undeniable logic to this. If an educator thinks something is important, necessary or relevant then they will naturally assess it; there will be a need to 'know and understand it', by noticing it, celebrating it and, ultimately, as a result of this, weaving their provision and pedagogy to provide for it. It is important so we should know about it. Alternatively, if we don't consider something to be important, relevant or 'significant' to children's learning and outcomes, then we are unlikely to asses, notice or celebrate it. If that is the case, then why would we seek to provide and facilitate it through our pedagogy and provision?

So the content of what children do is not neutral or 'naturally arrived at'. This content is carefully considered, decided upon and often passionately argued over. There is a good reason for this, because as practitioners and educators we bear the responsibility for ensuring that the children we work with develop and secure the knowledges, understandings and skills they will need in order to be successful participants in the society they live in. In order to fulfil this responsibility we take decisions about *what* this should be. We decide, as a society, as a community, what children need to *know* in order to be successful and participate. These 'bodies of content' define what we think is important and therefore what we will facilitate through pedagogy and, critically for this consideration, what we will assess.

The decisions that influence this are defined by many things, and what we consider to be important can change quite dramatically. For example, any responsible curriculum, the expression of this 'body of knowledge', would include the understanding and use of Information and Communication Technology (ICT) as a key skill. The world we live in, and the world today's children will enter as adults, is highly dependent on knowledge, understanding and confidence with ICT in order to function successfully. Therefore, to enable children to understand ICT and thus enable them to be part of this world – whatever our individual philosophy may incline us towards – is generally a part of the 'body of content' that is contained in some way within the provision and approaches, and assessing its use is a critical part of the pedagogical response. However, this was not always the case, and as recently as the 1980s computers played no part in the general curriculum, ICT was not taught as a basic necessity, and there was certainly no expectation that this would be a required skill for every citizen. As the world changes, as ideas, knowledges, technologies and understandings develop, change, reconfigure and appear, so these 'bodies of knowledge' alter and adapt in order to provide what upcoming generations will require. Inevitably, as both Carr and Broadfoot assert, this will impact on assessment.

Writing in 1992, Vic Kelly's overview of concepts on assessment refers to its imprecision and inappropriateness in trying to 'measure' attainment and achievement. However, here too there is an affirmation of assessment as the result of a personal judgement and this is, in turn, highly dependent on knowledge and experience and information. Although there is an attempt to prevent what is described as 'assessment being the master of the curriculum' there is again an acknowledgement that this relationship is by necessity an intrinsic one.

Equally, Geva Blenkin notes that a *subject-led curriculum*, and therefore assessment, runs counter to Early Years knowledge and practice (Blenkin 1992) and warns of the inevitable increase in inappropriate accountability and the increasing political agenda which then defines the assessment model for simplistic rather than authentic reasons. These were indeed prophetic words, yet it cannot be dismissed that even these statements, as accurate, insightful and reflective of an integrity as they are, come also from a set of beliefs and values about what any kind of content *should* consist of.

Carr and Lee (2012) cite Bourdieu and the notion of 'habitus', this being 'systems of durable, transposable dispositions' that inscribe 'things to do or not to do, things to say or not to say in relation to a probable upcoming future' (2012: 2). Again, we take decisions, carefully and through the medium of culture, expectations and values (to which I will return) to enshrine what we define as important. This 'significance' weaves through the curriculum content and therefore becomes inevitably and inextricably linked, driven by and responsible to the *content* of what is assessed, that is, known, understood and 'noticed', before it is then used.

The role of process

It is also important to establish that this content – the body of knowledge, skills and understanding – is a part, and by no means the whole, of the process and purpose. Alongside and parallel to this is the process of learning itself – learning and thinking *behaviours* and skills and the means by which children utilise, internalise and apply the content base to their everyday lives. Ultimately, these aspects of learning inject reality and purpose into the content base and are, on balance, at least equally, if not more important.

Säljö (1979) identifies five categories of learning; exploring the notion of 'deep' and 'surface level' learning and the interdependency that exists between them. While it could be argued that the first three categories refer to the 'bodies of content', they have no context, connection or application without the final two, and for 'deep learning', that which is truly significant, these final two categories become critical and therefore subject to a view and approach in terms of assessment:

1. Learning as a **quantitative increase in knowledge**. Learning is acquiring information or 'knowing a lot'.
2. Learning as **memorising**. Learning is storing information that can be reproduced.
3. Learning as acquiring facts, skills and methods that can be **retained and used as necessary**.
4. Learning as **making sense** or abstracting meaning. Learning involves relating parts of the subject matter to each other and to the real world.
5. Learning as interpreting and **understanding reality in a different way**. Learning involves comprehending the world by re-interpreting knowledge. (Säljö 1979)

For example, a concept of number is a knowledge base and a skill that we consider to be important. The ability to count permeates every aspect of daily life; so we designate it as something that children need to be taught, something that they need to learn and be confidently familiar with and therefore something that will ultimately comprise aspects of assessment. We need to know and understand children's concept and understanding of number in order to support and develop it. As practitioners we facilitate this leaning in a range of ways, finding practical and meaningful contexts to count in and shape children's understanding of its purpose. Alongside this we directly teach the numeric code and the associated skills of counting, such as 1 to 1 correspondence and the invariance of number. This might take place through directed adult-focused teaching sessions, through number rhymes, songs, stories and so on. We pass on the technical knowledge of the numeric code in this way. However, this remains abstract and detached for children until they begin to use it in their play and their everyday lives. So, the child who goes into the outdoor area and draws three circles, one for each of the bikes, is demonstrating an internalised, contextualised understanding of 1 to 1 correspondence. Similarly, the child preparing a picnic who counts out the number of plates and says that they need one more so that everyone will have one, has equally applied their knowledge of the mathematical code and skills to an everyday situation. The crucial point here is that not only is the 'content' known and familiar, but its application and purpose is fully understood and utilised.

It also follows that during the process of assessment 'how' children are assessed and the process by which they demonstrate significant learning behaviours is also acknowledged, understood and addressed. Similar to the principle that we pass on bodies of content that we consider to be important, the method and manner in which assessment takes place provide vital precepts and signposts to children about what is important about the way they use skills and knowledge as well as the content of what it actually is. Again, this is not a neutral process and how assessment is approached and understood is wholly underpinned by our own deeply held beliefs and values about the importance of the process and application of learning. Assessment demonstrates clear messages – that children will quickly and astutely internalise – about what we think learning is and what is important about what children do; it is a signifier of our own perception of learning and this has implications for children.

Assessment and values

Carr (2001) is clear that it is values and beliefs, not just what we know, that inform our perceptions and aspirations for children. We can believe that learning is linear and accumulative or we can believe that learning is complex, unpredictable and idiosyncratic. Essentially, we construct our own perception of children through how 'democratic' we believe the outcome and resulting dispositions should be.

Although theory and knowledge of children's development are obviously intertwined with this, and in turn are significantly influenced and shaped by experience, knowledge and on-going reflection as a professional, it is still primarily the 'value prism' which is both the starting point and the driver for decisions during the assessment process. Kelly (1992) again reasserts assessment as the essential element of the educational process, citing Hargreaves (1989), 'assessment more than curriculum or pedagogy has been the prime focal point of educational change' (Kelly 1992: 99) and noting that there can be no practice without theory.

Hurst and Lally (1992) are emphatic in regarding the impact of assessment as not merely on the curriculum content but on our *knowledge* of children and the procedures we follow to obtain our perceptions of learning. Evidently this influences how we *see* children and defines consequent decisions about what will be considered as 'signifiers' and 'significances'. As Hurst and Lally assert, 'Assessment is closely related to ... the evolution of ideas about educational quality as well as to the development of appropriate curricula' (1992: 46). They also state that 'Quality of educational experience for each child depends on the way in which assessment informs the curriculum'. Again this comes back not solely to a defined knowledge base, but to the value laden interpretation of assessment coupled with the confidence of practitioners to follow this without the diversions of short-term politics; a theme we will return to in Chapter 5.

So, the process of assessment shapes perceptions of children as learners and creates clear indicators of what is significant. In addition to this it clearly defines relationships between practitioners and children and between practitioners and other adults, particularly parents. The use and status of assessment within these relationships impacts directly on children as learners and on their identity (Carr 2001). There is, for example, a critical and undeniable need not to assess children in a clinical detached way but to understand the complexities of their learning and development, and the individual and unexpected journeys and trajectories that this can often take. (Hutchin 1999). Particularly critical is also ensuring that parental involvement is both genuine and not restricted to delivering a setting-based view of expected learning. We know that children respond differently to different adults in different situations and, therefore, if we are serious about the authenticity of assessment, this will mean taking a much broader, wider and flexible view than that of the practitioner alone.

Part of the rationale for this could be argued to be purely pragmatic, in that it provides the most effective route to all-round authentic information. Yet alongside this are key principles, again, value based, which centre the child as the agent of their learning and the empowerment of self-identity that accompanies this (Carr and Lee 2012). This self-perception and construction of identity, a central concern of Margaret Carr's work, is explicit in the assessment process, and she refers to the need to support the construction of this identity as one of the '... consequences for assessment practice', going on to state that 'Assessment for learning plays a powerful role in this early construction of learner identity' (Carr and Lee 2012: 1).

Understanding and acknowledging the 'under the surface' nature of the implications of process influences the key considerations within this dimension.

- Do parents contribute to assessments? Do practitioners seek their input when considering their view of the child as a learner? The message here is again an obvious one about value and the importance of the parents' role as both primary caregiver and first – and most enduring – educator. The wealth of information not acknowledged would prove highly detrimental to the accuracy of any overall conclusions.

- Do children contribute to their own assessment? Do we as practitioners recognise the emerging importance of children's self-awareness and self-perception and the equally vital role of their 'metacognition' – knowing how they know what they know (Whitebread 2012)? Again, not utilising this not only diminishes the overall picture but misses an opportunity to develop a tangible vehicle for developing children's ability and skill at 'knowing how to learn'.

- Traditionally contentious is the tension between observational assessment and test-based assessment. The purpose of mentioning this here is not to explore the empirical detail but to examine the values that underpin it. What do we say to children when we test them to find out what they know? What do we say about the value of their play, their self-discoveries and their self-initiated activity if this is never taken into account?

The decisions we take, the judgements we make, the assessments we select to notice and act upon are all the result of values and beliefs that we hold as practitioners . This 'value prism', although appearing to be neutral and objective, is in fact highly subjective and determinant. Olson and Bruner (1996) refer to 'folk pedagogy' in a manner akin to Carr's (2001) 'folklore model of assessment'. They state that 'everyday intuitive theories and models reflect deeply ingrained cultural beliefs and assumptions' (Olson and Bruner 1996 in Carr 2001). Although these are informed by experience and reflection, they begin from an initial origin that defines the purpose and aspirations for what we do and strongly influences all our actions, thoughts, decisions and ideas.

Clarke (2001) states that as educators we take these decisions early in our career (if not before, in which case they may ultimately be responsible for the career choice itself) and proceed to refine, adapt and utilise them as we progress and gain experience. In the intensely politically influenced field of education it is not unusual for these values and beliefs to become concealed by the 'cognitive and moral clutter' of government initiatives, expectations and politically motivated educational decisions.

It is also important to be aware that the values we hold are often strongly culturally defined (Whitebread 2012). Carr and Lee (2012) use the definition created by Nasir et al. in order to define this: 'By culture we mean the constellation of practices historically developed and dynamically shaped by communities in order to accomplish the purposes they value' (in Carr and Lee 2012: 4).

So our values reflect cultural expectations and mores, and draw from the impact of all influences that have historically shaped a belief or value at this point in time. There is no escape from the subjectivity of this, nor, as I have argued, is it possible to be 'value free' or objective, especially in the area of Early Childhood assessment. The point is to define these values and be clear about what they are; so that at an incidence of possible 'clutter' they can be reasserted, re-established and replenished. This then enables us to retain the core responsibility for what we do as Early Years practitioners, and enables us to be clear, determined, justified, and indeed accountable for the actions and decisions we choose to undertake.

So let us define what these values are, might be and could be. In an exploration of this subject, Lloyd-Yero (2010) acknowledges how every action is built on values and pleads for an increased awareness that educators formally identify them. There is also an understanding of the uniqueness of this for individual educators, noting that 'Even if a "list" of cultural values existed, each teacher would possess his or her own "take" on those values'. The definition of this is as follows:

> Values are principles, qualities, or objects that a person perceives as having intrinsic worth. Every individual has a personal hierarchy of values that may include success, wealth or monetary comfort, love/companionship, a sense of accomplishment or achievement, and of course, survival. The choices we make reflect what we value the most at a particular point in time. When people possess what they value, they are contented. If they are deprived of what they value, they feel frustration or dissatisfaction. Humans, therefore, unconsciously behave in ways that move them toward what they value or away from anything counter to that value. (Lloyd-Yero 2010)

Best (quoted in Lloyd-Yero 2010) too notes that:

> If we – or others – are to judge how effective any teaching experience has been, then it's essential to uncover the values underpinning that experience and the intended outcomes that stem from them. The starting point is surely to examine the values that form the foundation of your own teaching.

He goes on differentiate two specific types of values that relate to this:

- general values associated with the processes of education
- the more specific values underlying effective teaching. (Best 2012)

I shall deal with the second aspect in more detail as part of Chapter 5 as this, I believe, concerns itself more with our 'knowledge of what works' and the process of how children become effective learners. There is an overlap here between science and philosophy/belief that I will explore then. For now, I would like to focus primarily on the first value – the process, or purpose, of education and how this is underpinned by values and what they might be.

These values have often been incorporated into, or indeed cited as foundations for approaches, curricula, outcomes and pedagogies. Notable examples of this are: Te Whariki, the pre-schools of Reggio Emilia, the International Baccalaureate, the English National Curriculum (2000) and the English Early Years Foundation Stage (2008).

However, as I have discussed, this is often reinterpreted and modified on an individual and collective basis. As an Early Years Adviser and Consultant I would often begin training sessions with an exploration of the participants' values under the umbrella question of 'what do we want for children?'. Single words would then be collected and shared with the group. Although this is not an empirical study, the results of this, regardless of the geography, community, age, experience or qualifications of the practitioner, would be universally similar and a broad consensus would always be apparent. The values that practitioners wanted for the children in their setting and which were reflective and indicative of the 'kind of future' (Postman 1982) they would strive for, were continually cited within the following broad headings:

Independence and the ability for children to take control of their own learning by having their own ideas and the self-assurance to follow interests, projects and fascinations was seen as an important way in which children begin the process of empowering themselves as learners. There are often concerns that the 'learned helplessness' which often characterised traditional, behaviourist approaches to early education did not instil the qualities of self-reliance that are considered to be crucial for lifelong success. This value of supporting young children to begin to take their own decisions and access tools, resources and materials by themselves is a staple aspect of value-driven pedagogy.

Confidence, that is the self-belief and self-assurance that drives the energy and commitment to achieve, communicate and participate, was often the first value-driven 'aspiration' for children that practitioners voiced. Much of achievement and innate drive rests on the confidence that challenges can be addressed and successfully accomplished. The careful nurturing of confidence, self-belief and the harnessing of everything known and understood to achieve a goal underpins much of lifelong learning and success across all areas. To participate in society, to communicate, to shape ideas and innovations requires a belief, a level of self-esteem, that expects or believes that this can happen.

Curiosity and enthusiasm for learning were seen as vital traits to encourage and support in children. The idea of 'lifelong learning' as a constant, continual process, and that as practitioners we 'teach children how to learn' is vital in ensuring that children continue their quest for knowledge and skills and that there is always implicit in what they did a refined and secured 'love of learning'. The curiosity, to find out, discover, understand, wonder and explore were seen as things that lay at the very core of not just good academic outcomes but heightened life chances and the pursuit of happiness and fulfilment.

Critical thinking – it is no accident that the world renowned pre-schools of Reggio Emilia were historically founded as a direct response to the Italian experience of Fascism under Mussolini. One of the founding principles was that Fascism should never happen in Italy again, and therefore children would need to grow up learning how to challenge, question and participate fully in society. A key quality for future citizens, and one that will have a direct bearing on the kind of society they create, will be their ability and confidence to be critical and analyse and question aspects of that society. It was felt by Early Years practitioners that far from accepting things at face value, disempowered and detached from society and unable to challenge aspects of decision making, a key aspiration for children was to be active participants in an inclusive accountable democracy.

Responsibility was considered to be an important value for citizenship and a society that functions harmoniously. Within this as an umbrella term, is encompassed traits such as empathy, care, a sense of justice, and an understanding of the need for mutual respect and co-operation. A sense of taking responsibility for one's own actions and being responsible for those around us resonates very strongly with Ferre Leavers' sense of 'Linkedness' (the absence of which he argues is 'delinquency'). Shaped as both a pragmatic and philosophical virtue, many practitioners cited this as one of their most fundamental values and aspirations for the children in their setting.

Reflectiveness – the ability to reflect on one's own ideas, approaches and decisions – was also highly valued and considered to be an important outcome for children. The ability to internalise and analyse thoughts, ideas and actions was believed to be important as this enabled learners to make more complex and creative links, refine and re-work what they knew and develop this even further. As a value this was strongly linked to the importance of what is sometimes referred to as 'thinking skills' and links strongly with the notion and development of creativity in all aspects of life.

Ability to self-regulate – developmental psychologists are clear that the skill required to manage feelings and emotions is a critical determinant of on-going and later success (Whitebread 2012). It is important to be able to reflect on emotions and make decisions from this position, and to critically be able to deny instant gratification. The famous Wikart Study's 'Cookie test' (Schweinhart et al. 2005) is an evident example of this where children able to 'see beyond the immediate' were more likely to be able to manage and regulate their emotions and feelings, and were thus able to curb impetuosity and take calmer, more reflective and considered decisions that would affect the nature of their outcomes.

Risk taking – in order for society and civilisation to progress, for new ideas, technologies, inventions and understandings to occur; risks have to be taken. Entrepreneurs will say that calculated risk lies at the heart of all innovation. What was felt is that children need to contribute to their success with an ability to calculate the nature of risk and offset it against the potential outcome. This was heavily predicated on the important notion that we learn from our mistakes and trying different things, and that a 'right answer fixation' would be detrimental to this. Thus a culture of trying, and indeed the necessity for failure, needed to be part of the value base.

The ability to make connections is a vital cognitive function that enables learners to 'draw upon' existing experiences, knowledges and skills. Children's learning is rarely self-separated into the constructed areas and disciplines of traditional 'curriculum areas'; instead children exist in and focus on the moment and the specific outcome in hand. For example, this could be expressing and communicating an idea, representing an experience or solving a problem. Children with the ability to make connections will trawl experiences and memories in order to apply and utilise existing skills and knowledge to support the development or conclusion of their self-motivated project.

Creativity was identified as one of the single most important values on which pedagogy is based and that aspirations are driven by. It has been widely accepted that the concept of creativity is a fundamental aspect of development and progress and is not limited to the traditional definitions that restrict it to what might be described as 'The Arts'. Creative thinking, the ability to think 'out of the box' and to approach all aspects of life and learning in a way that negotiates obstacles and finds new and innovative means of addressing issues was identified as a key factor for higher possibilities of success.

Communication in a range of different forms was also considered to be a critical skill and a key value. In order to participate in society, the ability to express ideas, thoughts, feelings and opinions and to communicate was believed to be vital. Partially it was felt that this stemmed initially from an articulacy in language and the ability to express oneself. There is much evidence that links this with self-esteem and confidence in addition to the neurological connection between language and memory. Additionally it was felt that other dimensions of communication, underpinned by the same principles, were also important for self-awareness, reflection and participation.

Tenacity and persistence, the ability or trait to keep going, overcome difficulties and setbacks, try different things and manage the frustration of denial and lack of resolution were again seen as vital life skills and important values that should underpin a responsible pedagogy. There is a maxim that 'nothing worth knowing reveals itself easily', and this can often lie at the heart of successful and effective learning and development. Much of what we are confronted with as life unfolds requires 'stickability' and a persistence to continue. Much of life's successes – academic, emotional and economic – rely heavily on the ability to persist.

... and finally:

To be skilled and knowledgeable, though technically not a 'value' or 'belief' in the same sense, was considered to be important as this referred to the 'habitus' (quoted in Carr 2001) of what we pass on to children in terms of collective knowledge and skills that are required in order to be successful in the society and community in which they live. In this exercise it was always stressed by the participants that possession of these skills and knowledge (the previously referred to content base) was not enough in itself and the previous values or aspirations were critically important in order to enable these skills and knowledge to have a context, a meaning and a clear purpose. Säljö's (1979) identification of the five categories of learning (see page 22) explicitly refers to this as the relationship between the first three and the final two categories.

 Reflective task

Identify your own values as a practitioner. What are the skills, qualities, knowledges and understandings that you aspire for the children that you work with? How are they reflected in your pedagogy and approaches to assessment?

Further reading

Blenkin, G.M. and Kelly, A.V. (1992) *Assessment in Early Childhood Education*. London: Paul Chapman.
Carter, C. and Nutbrown, C. (2013) 'The tools of assessment: Watching and learning', in G. Pugh and B. Duffy (eds), *Contemporary Issues in Early Years*, 6th edition. London: SAGE.

3

What are the Purposes of Assessment?

This chapter will:

• Explore the different ways assessment is presented and the range of uses to which it is applied

• Provide a critical overview of the nature of measurement and data

• Define and explore the nature of formative and summative assessment

• Identify a range of terminology and language used in association with the uses of assessment information

• Explore the nature of internal and external accountability in Early Years provision

So far we have established a definition of assessment as an on-going pedagogical behaviour that importantly underpins, defines and embodies values and beliefs about children and their learning. Its impact on shaping that understanding, and the content and approach to curriculum and pedagogy has also been explored.

It is now important to shift the perspective to look in more detail at the 'pragmatic' and tangible aspect of assessment and review in detail its 'purpose' on a more outwardly facing level. What does and should happen to the information we process about the children we work with? How is it understood and, most importantly, how is it, and how should it be used?

The Assessment Reform Group's (2002) definition of using assessment data is a useful starting point. It states that 'The process of seeking and interpreting evidence for use by learners and their teachers to decide where the learners are in their learning, where they need to go next, and how best to get there'.

As previously discussed, Drummond (1993) describes assessment as posing and answering three questions; the last of which, having seen what there is to see and hear, and having made sense of and interpreted it, is asking ourselves: 'how do we put our understanding to good use?'

Hutchin (1996) elaborates on this: 'The purpose of the assessment process is to make explicit children's achievements, celebrate their achievements with them, and *help them to move forward to the next goal*' (1996: 7, my emphasis).

This reveals aspects regarding values and beliefs about children and indeed outcomes; the 'goals' Hutchin refers to have to be defined as outcomes, implicitly or explicitly, and may refer to 'bodies of content' or learning and thinking behaviours', as previously discussed. In addition, this explores the importance of focusing on the unique and individual journey, trajectory and pace, the importance of **achievement** rather than pure **attainment** – something I will return to later – and it also asserts that assessment is a **process**, not a single event or series of separate unattached and unrelated events.

More pertinent to this discussion, assessment is defined as consisting of dynamic, live and valid information; not to be statically recorded, or objectively 'viewed' but ultimately feeding into and driving learning, teaching and pedagogy, defining and identifying next steps, future trajectories and 'signifiers' and/or 'significances' in learning.

Measurement and data

As with any information that is used for any purpose, its usefulness and 'applicability' is entirely dependent on its accuracy and validity. One of the challenges in Early Years assessment is establishing that authenticity of what, as Drummond (1993) would say, is 'seen and understood'. In later chapters we will continue to explore the notion of what is 'significant' and what aspects of children's learning and development are visible, viewable and understandable. However, there are continual tensions between the 'reality' of children and what is easily 'measurable'. Many broader and what might be described as 'strategic' approaches to assessment rely heavily on 'measuring' in some way what children are demonstrating, and ultimately providing scores or numerical representations of outcomes and 'significances'. This is fraught with tensions and contradictions, not least because of what we know about the way children learn and develop, and how they demonstrate this (see Chapter 4), but also because the science itself is an imprecise one, and one that owes more to convenience and expediency than accuracy, validity and honesty.

Kelly (1992) notes that:

> Assessment is often spoken of as educational measurement ... The term measurement brings with it connotations of precision and accuracy. Yet ... there is little that is precise or accurate about most forms of assessment in education and thus (it needs to be acknowledged) that it can seldom, if ever, be regarded as measurement in any mathematical sense of the term.

She goes on to say:

> Accuracy of assessment is related inversely to the complexity and the sophistication of what is being assessed. And since education is a highly complex and sophisticated process, educational assessment can be regarded as measurement only in the remotest of metaphorical senses. (Kelly 1992: 4)

This has immense implications for some of the processes and uses of assessment that we will discuss later in this chapter, particularly when the stakes, assumptions and consequences of this are so significant.

It is also important at this juncture to define and clarify the use of the word 'data'. The assumption made, especially in some parts of the Early Years community, is that this immediately declares itself to be a combination of numbers, mathematical formulas and abstract calculations; in precisely the misguided and dishonest way that Kelly refers to above. It is important to be clear that this is not the case, and the term data simply refers to information. This is not merely an indulgent semantic point, as in exploring issues around Early Years assessment, its nature, purpose and outcomes, the issue of accountability continually surfaces. In discussing this, effort needs to be made to appropriate the language and terminology in a way that supports and describes what we know and believe to be important, significant and authentic. It is neither useful nor appropriate to dismiss an aspect of language, such as the term 'data', because of a discomfort that this might invoke. Rather we should take ownership of it, redefine and utilise it to confront misuse with the appropriate linguistic tools.

So, we know that learning, development, pedagogy and provision are inextricably linked; I would argue that this is through the process of broadly defined assessment as the knowing and understanding of children to create and support the possibilities for their future. Assessment is the dynamic process of interpreting information – data – and then using this to develop outcomes and understanding of how this can be most effectively facilitated.

Formative and summative assessments

The uses – and indeed the misuses – of assessment data are broad and varied. However, the simple starting point is that of differentiating and understanding the uses and definitions of 'formative' and 'summative' assessment.

As previously referred to, Clarke (2001) provides a starting point for exploring the distinction between them that is worth repeating:

> We think of our children as plants ... summative assessment of plants is the process of simply measuring them. The measurement might be interesting to compare and analyse, but in themselves they do not affect the growth of plants. Formative assessment, on the other hand, is the garden equivalent of feeding and watering the plants, directly affecting their growth. (2001: 2)

Formative assessment is translating information directly into how we respond to, interact with, provide and plan for children's learning and development. It is the active process of identifying the 'invisible moments of possibility' that exist sometimes momentarily and sometimes with intense vulnerability. Effective practitioners are aware of these; they 'tune into' them and then act accordingly through their knowledge and 'value prism'. Formative assessment is noticing and observing patterns of behaviour, interests, approaches and ideas that children demonstrate, and shaping the environment, activities and themes or projects in order to support and enhance them. It is through this process of formative assessment that practitioners enact their responsibility as professionals to ensure that children's development proceeds towards greater mastery and that they have appropriate opportunity for challenge (Bredekamp and Copple 1997). Formative assessment is the on-going pedagogical behaviour, often intuitive or sometimes counter-intuitive, and it is always directly informed by knowledge of the child, their needs and a suitable framework for development. It specifically and skilfully informs understanding of and planning for the group or the individual by identifying strengths and areas of development.

Summative assessment collects all information, at any point in time, and summarises achievement, attainment, interests, learning behaviours and interests. Critically, especially if we are to move away from the false and dishonest 'measurement' of children, this will incorporate both a summary of their knowledge, in terms of 'bodies and content', and also their 'learning and thinking behaviours'. To re-reference Säljö (1979), (see p. 22) it requires an acknowledgement of all five categories of learning definitions. A professional judgement is made by the practitioner as to the information that is relevant, accurate and necessary. A summative assessment might be closely aligned to specific criteria, or put in the context of a particular set of expectations, aspirations or outcomes. Equally, a summative assessment may be a more open-ended and holistic overview of the child at a given point in time: a narrative, portfolio or 'Learning Journey'.

Kelly (1992) also notes that as well as being formative and summative, assessments can also be:

- **Diagnostic** – to identify and classify learning difficulties so that appropriate support can be targeted. A diagnostic assessment would include references and seek advice from external specialist agencies to identify and support specifically identified needs.

- **Evaluative** – to view outcomes strategically in order to enable accountability.

Blenkin (1992) also adds a series of subdivisions that identify specific aspects of the structure and portrayal of different types of assessment. Again, understanding these are vital when considering the applicability and the uses and misuses of assessment, and particularly the necessity for such data to be reliable, accurate, honest and meaningful.

- **Norm referenced or standardised assessment** – works on the principle of a clearly established expectation, benchmark or 'norm'. Children either meet the expectation or they do not and often assumptions and conclusions are drawn from this. Typically these assessments work in a formal/adult-directed rather than observational context and are viewed as a 'clinical' approach to understanding attainment.

- **Criterion referenced assessment** – is closely linked to particular curricula foci and gauges whether specific items of knowledge are known or specific skills can be demonstrated. These often follow a particular focus and the purpose is to assess the impact of the teaching/provision on the immediate and short-term understanding of the recipient.

- **Ipsative assessment** – is, in contrast to the previous two examples, a *qualitative* rather than a *quantitative* assessment, in that it is not related to any norm or specific criteria. This type of approach and outcome relate wholly to a child's specific starting point and development in a range of ways. In contrast to being an assessment against a 'norm', 'expectation' or indeed in relation to the outcomes produced by other children, this type of assessment is, in effect, an assessment 'against oneself'.

As we have previously discussed, effective assessment is accurate and valid and based on interpreting on-going knowledge built up by practitioners, and it is an essential prerequisite for meeting children's needs as unique and individual learners. Hurst and Lally (1992) rightly assert that for any 'curriculum' to be relevant and applicable it has to be 'personalised' to ensure that this can happen. Only specific and equally individual assessment that forms the next steps in the journey is capable of doing this.

It follows then that when considering assessment in any form and for any purpose, its primary function is always within the realms of 'formative assessment'. Although other uses may be made of this information – and we will discuss these in a moment – if such information is not wholly for the benefit of understanding children's learning and development in order to support their future trajectory then serious questions need to be asked. As Fisher points out: 'The quality of summative assessment relies on the quality of formative assessment' (2008: 168). Additionally, if the purpose of assessment is anything other than formative – literally 'forming and shaping the learning possibilities' – then it will have potentially dire consequences on the process involved in obtaining the information, its status and, especially if the stakes are high, its ultimate validity and honesty. Hurst and Lally state that 'Properly understood assessment puts the achievement of the learner at the centre of the educational process' (1992: 46). The veracity of the statement, although patently obvious, can often get lost underneath other more 'strategic' and 'formulaic' requirements, calculations and expectations. It is the continual responsibility of the practitioner to question who, or what else, *should* be at the centre of the process. Given what we understand about the uniqueness of child development, progress and learning (further explored in Chapter 4) there is a strong argument for the approach defined in the concept of 'ipsative assessment' to be located at the core of all assessment purposes.

Practitioners respond to children's needs with 'informed intuition' recognising the 'signifiers of learning' and filtering the significance, both in terms of interest, motivation and understanding, and, as an educator with aspirations and outcomes, in terms of what might be possible next, with respect to 'knowledge and skill content' and 'learning and thinking behaviours'.

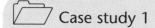

Case study 1

Emily, aged 14 months, sits with the content of an exploratory basket that she has investigated around her. She begins to show a particular interest in putting small objects like shells and pebbles into some of the small containers and carefully collects and arranges them to make this easier. As she fills them, they overflow and she cannot put any more in. Her carer brings some bigger containers and places these alongside. Emily transfers the objects into the larger receptacles and begins to sort them so that the same objects are together.

Case study 2

Sam – a 3-year-old 'reluctant writer' – has found a worm in the outdoor area and excitedly shows it to the practitioner. In the ensuing conversation he proudly states that he will keep it in his pocket until he gets home to show everyone in his family. Further discussion with the practitioner follows and Sam eventually agrees, with some reluctance, that this would not be kind to the worm. However, seeing his interest and motivation, the practitioner identifies this as a 'moment of possibility' and gives him a spiral bound notebook, telling him that he could record this find in there, and show everyone that instead. Sam silently nods and takes the notebook. He washes his hands and puts the worm in a petri dish and draws it. Over the next few days the book becomes full of objects and items he has found outside, all carefully recorded, with the beginnings of non-standard writing appearing to label his finds.

Case study 3

Ruksaad is painting a picture of a recent trip to the seaside. She has already made the figures that represent the members of her family who were there. She wants to make the background by using a wash for the sand, sea and sky. However, she starts to become frustrated because the blue she has mixed is the same, so the sky and sea are indistinguishable from each other. Noticing this, the practitioner starts to talk about the differences in colour between them and Ruksaad remembers that the sky was lighter and the sea much darker than the blue she has mixed. The practitioner shows her how to mix in black or white paint to darken or lighten the colour and Ruksaad enjoys perfecting this until she is happy that the result is accurate.

Having established the formative aspect as the main purpose and function of assessment, it is also necessary to acknowledge that the summative dimension, although clearly secondary in status, can also perform an important and valuable role in enabling practitioners to inform, reflect on and develop their practice.

Summarising children learning at a point in time and reflecting on and analysing the data this produces, practitioners are enabled to make clear and informed judgements both about the individual children on a wider, more 'macro' level and also about the effect and effectiveness of their practice and provision on the children as a group.

As opposed to the more 'purist' formative aspect, described as reacting to individual situations and 'nudging learning forward' (Fisher 2008), summative assessment is a broader overview, considered carefully and with decisions taken that influence the learning environment, the nature of interaction and what might be described as 'curriculum delivery' in addition to the support for learning and thinking 'behaviours'.

Nutbrown (2001: 69) notes that observations 'provide starting points for reviewing the effectiveness of provision ... and can be used to identify strengths, weaknesses, gaps and inconsistencies'. She goes on to assert that this can 'illuminate the future' by exploring 'the possible outcomes of provision ... the curriculum, pedagogy, interactions and relationships'.

The principle of interpreting 'what there is to see' (Drummond 1993) and acting on the information remains the same, but in the process of summative assessment this looks beyond the immediate 'moments of possibility' and towards a broader more longitudinal future trajectory.

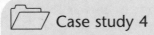 Case study 4

> The practitioner working with Sophia, who is 18 months old, has identified her interest in rotational schemas; she makes large circles in paint and mark-making materials, moves objects such as small world animals in large circles around her and turns herself around in the outdoor area. Her parents have noticed this at home too, being intrigued by her sudden interest in the washing machine in full spin cycle. The practitioner provides a range of additional resources with which she can continue to explore this, encouraging her to mix materials in a bucket, stirring for food preparation, exploring wheeled objects in a range of situations and swinging her around in the outdoor area.

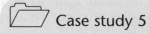 Case study 5

Two children aged 3 are exploring cornflour in a large tray and begin to discuss its various qualities. The practitioner begins to interact with them and they start to identify the changes in its substance as they manipulate it. Both children become very interested in the way it changes and the practitioner skilfully introduces key vocabulary to describe what is happening. Identifying the children's motivation and interest as an opportunity to continue developing their language, the practitioner enhances the malleable materials area of provision with a range of other types of dough and other materials. The practitioner ensures that, when appropriate, an adult interacts to supply additional vocabulary.

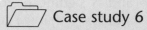 Case study 6

In the outdoor area of a Reception class, Max is fascinated with chalking pathways for the wheeled toys to move around and often spends time creating different routes which are faithfully followed by the other children. Over the next few days, the practitioner augments the resources with laminated directional signs which are taped to small cones. Max discusses the best places for these to go and sets about extending the complexity of the routes. Additionally, a small electronic traffic light is used which Max then controls to regulate the flow of traffic. Throughout this process Max's understanding is supported and challenged through conversation with the practitioner.

Additionally, the process of summative assessment provides a critical vehicle for discussing and exchanging information with parents and carers to ensure that a clear, unified and self-supportive approach is both discussed and utilised.

Different kinds of accountability

Any discussion of summative assessment inevitably leads to an exploration of the notion of accountability. Again, this is a word that is often (understandably) loaded with negative baggage and viewed in a purely pejorative sense by many practitioners. However, it is important to understand that, firstly, this accountability can take different forms, internal and external, and I will discuss the nature of both and how summative assessment relates to these. Secondly, and perhaps more importantly, it is also crucial to assert that accountability is a key feature of our responsibility as practitioners. What we do, on a day-to-day basis, changes children's lives. This is an inevitable consequence of being a significant adult in the life of a child. What we do as practitioners either empowers children as learners, or it doesn't; it equips them with the skills, knowledge and understanding to be successful in life, or it doesn't; we enable them as thinkers, doers, innovators and responsible critical citizens – or we don't. In short, we either empower children as learners that are active within all five of Säljö's categories, or we don't; (see p. 22) we achieve the shared values and broad outcomes and aspirations we have as practitioners (discussed in Chapter 2), or we don't. The issue is not whether we should be made accountable or not, but to *whom* we are accountable and *what* we are accountable *for*. Central to this discussion, and further explored in the next chapter, is the *'what'* we should be accountable for, in terms of what matters and is significant for children. I believe that it is true – or certainly should be – that we are accountable to and for the children we work with, and in that respect we take decisions as informed professionals in terms of what that is and how it is affected through practice, provision and pedagogy.

As practitioners, our **internal accountability** is not just a personal perception of the impact or success of our practice, but a professional reflection and discussion as to whether we can be 'the best we can be'; after all, this is what will make the most difference to children's outcomes and possibilities. In this way, our summative assessments give us the overview to make critical judgements on our own practice and provision. It gives us the data – information – and opportunity to judge whether or not children are 'moving in predictable direction towards greater mastery' (Bredekamp and Copple 1997), whether or not there are appropriate opportunities for challenge and development, and whether children have the opportunities to demonstrate what they know in their play and through self-initiated activity, either supported or unsupported by an adult. We can reflect on whether or not, as individuals or a group, children are acquiring the skills they need to be successful, and whether they have the opportunities to apply, explore and refine these in a range of contexts and situations. We can also ascertain whether their learning and thinking behaviours are shaping and supporting their development and understanding.

Effective practitioners continually refine and utilise this information – partly to inform their practice and modify their provision accordingly, but also partly to reassure and re-reference their own values and beliefs about children, learning and the purpose of education to ensure that their role and their impact is 'as good as it can possibly be'.

Alongside this runs the parallel vein of **external accountability**. As educators we are responsible for shaping and supporting the skills and knowledge of future generations; we are therefore accountable to society for this, as we are to the future. As recipients of public finance we have a responsibility to ensure that this finite resource is used effectively and purposefully; we are therefore also accountable for this. The issue is not whether or not we are externally accountable but the means by which this is derived and the dynamic between this and our own, professionally driven, internal accountability, that is based on our values and expertise as practitioners and our knowledge of who the children are and what they need to be successful.

It is a constant tension within the Early Years community that any discussions of external accountability rarely acknowledge this, or take the complex nature of children into account. Often, the measures for external accountability take the form of unrelated or spurious devices that can be easily collated and analysed. More often than not, such external accountabilities rely heavily on the notion of 'measuring' children's learning and development and consequently developing mathematical formulas for how this should be progressing, often resulting in targets and calculations of outcomes and trajectories of later attainment.

The issue of 'measurement' is a vexed an interesting one. In Chapter 4 we will discuss the nature of children's development and the significant aspects that require assessment to support on-going learning, support and challenge, as this relates strongly to the *nature* of such signifiers and whether identifying them requires, necessitates or even creates the possibility of measurement.

As previously quoted, Kelly (1992: 4) notes that 'there is little that is precise or accurate about most forms of assessment in education and thus (it needs to be acknowledged) that it can seldom, if ever, be regarded as measurement in any mathematical sense of the word'. She also states that 'in an age that calls itself scientific, it is an extraordinary fact that education is dominated by myth and superstition as was medicine before the Renaissance' (1992: 50).

Whereas the signifiers of children's learning are sometimes observable – visible, audible and apparent – they are not entities that can be quantifiable in the mathematical sense, albeit that some people would like the convenience of a simple graph or number from which decisions of accountability and effectiveness can be easily taken. Attempting to condense the complexity of young learners' development into a numerical score is a ludicrous and bizarre activity; it runs contrary to everything we know about children's development and contradicts the values and beliefs that most practitioners agree on. It is a valid question to ask at this juncture whether we can derive a 'score' for the quality of a thought, the warmth and understanding of a relationship, an assertion of confidence or the dynamic use of a word or phrase. It is not to say that these things are not 'assessable' – the opposite is the case – but how we describe them and how we *justify* them becomes the issue of contention. Where such 'scoring' exists it is evident that it does not reflect 'authentic' or even usable information and has simplified potentially valuable data to the point of bland, sterile and arid irrelevance.

Added to this is the sheer individuality and combination of genetic propensities, experiences, understandings and perceptions that combine to generate the uniqueness of every single individual learner. Kelly (1992: 5) reiterates this: '… one of the reasons why accurate assessment of educational attainment has proved impossible is that education, however one conceives it, is a highly personal matter since it involves human beings, every one of whom has his/her own characteristics'.

It is worth then considering the wider context in which the purpose(s) of assessment exists. There is a firm and compelling argument that the only starting point in this context should be how this revolves around the developmental and learning needs of children. Although this is an obvious stance to take, it is clear that this frequently and consistently gets diluted and buried under the simplified and sometimes spurious demands of forcefully driven external accountabilities.

We have discussed the important role that summative assessment plays as an aspect of on-going pedagogical behaviour and the critical role of practitioners' value driven, expertise-informed internal accountability. However, we must not forget that this is not 'assessment', but a sometimes useful and necessary by-product of the formative process. Blenkin and Kelly (1992: ix) state that 'summative assessment is external to (the assessment) process and functions not as an aid to educational advance but merely as an attempt to "measure" it and is thus best seen as a political rather than an educational device', and this immediately unravels the role and nature of huge swathes of external accountability that rely solely on different forms of summative assessment. These uses are *political* rather than educational; they are truncated, short-term views on policy impact and political credibility.

It is a strange double-edged (mis)fortune that, particularly in England since the late 1990s, there has been a sustained and dramatic interest in and attention to the importance of Early Years provision. In 1996, the 'Desirable Learning Outcomes', linked to a free, voucher-led, Early Years entitlement, was the forerunner for later, more sophisticated, extensive and statutory requirements to the Early Years through frameworks of the Foundation Stage Curriculum Guidance and the Early Years Foundation Stage framework. Governments since this time have realised and acted upon the impact of effective provision and pedagogy and the potentially lifelong benefits that can be gained from a high quality 'pre-school' experience (Sylva et al. 2010). Although this elevation in status was, and should have been welcomed, it has inevitably come at a price. In previous years, Early Years was considered far less important, existing at the lowest foothills compared to later primary and secondary education, the Himalayas of importance and status. Therefore little attention was paid to monitoring and accounting its impact. In this previous environment, practitioners and settings developed their own, principled, informed and value-led approaches that continued to develop undetected by wider concerns or expectations. With the new-found status of Early Years provision a plethora of measurements, expectations, targets and duties suddenly and vociferously evolved; to the point where successive governments (in addition to encroaching widespread interference in pedagogy) have sought to 'technicalise' the accountability for purely political purposes and subject Early Years provision to a 'laser beam' scrutiny that has invariably spawned a series of inappropriate, inaccurate and spurious measures.

The issue here, and an issue it certainly is, is the need for the Early Years community as a whole, as well as individual practitioners, to take ownership of the nature of accountability and ensure, forcefully where necessary, that its real purpose is supporting children and that this is never compromised or diluted by external demands or expectations. The impact of this has been, and will continue to be, catastrophic as it will undermine practitioner confidence and judgement – the very things required to ensure effectiveness. Carr (2001: 47) notes that '… as demands for external accountability press more insistently on the profession, surveillance begins to encroach on intuitive and responsive teaching'. This encroaching, widely recognisable, is a damaging and unnecessary drain on the purpose and effectiveness of Early Years practice.

There are three aspects concerning this to be aware of.

Firstly, there needs to be a clear and precise understanding that summative assessment is an outcome of formative assessment and not an entity in its own right; it must always be driven by the definition of assessment as knowing who the child is, what they know, what they can do and the kinds of learners they are.

Secondly, it is important that what practitioners are held accountable for is meaningful, purposeful and relevant to children's learning and development, not what is simply easily measureable. A quote attributed to Einstein sums up the paradox: 'Not everything that counts can be counted, and not everything that can be counted counts'.

Thirdly, ownership of this must be taken by practitioners themselves, and they should not wait for political agendas to drive outcomes and expectations. Hurst and Lally (1992: 47) note that 'Educational reasons are the only rational foundation for educational decisions. Our knowledge of the way children learn should be the determining force in educational policy ...'. This may mean challenging contradictions to this as they emerge and being clear about principles, values and realities.

Reflective task

How do the assessments you make influence and impact on your practice and provision? How does your knowledge and understanding of children influence your interactions and pedagogy? How does this impact on your planning and the environment you work in?

Further reading

Dowling, M. (1992) *Education 3–5: A Teacher's Handbook*. London: Paul Chapman.
Fisher, J. (2008) *Starting from the Child: Teaching and Learning*. Maidenhead: Open University Press.
Swaffield, S. (ed.) (2008) *Unlocking Assessment: Understanding for Reflection and Application*. London: David Fulton.

Significances and Signifiers of Child Development

This chapter will:

- Explore theories of how children learn
- Identify significant and relevant aspects of children's learning and development
- Examine the relationship between the process and content of children's learning

In the previous chapters we have explored the nature of assessment and the purposes – appropriate and otherwise – for which it is used. Its function as a key pedagogical behaviour to support, challenge and extend children's learning and development has been discussed. We have also defined its existence, located within the practitioner's individual 'value prism', and how this shapes and influences decisions and approaches that practitioners ultimately take when engaged in assessment as part of their everyday practice and provision.

I now intend to turn to identifying and exploring the 'content' of such assessment, by which I mean the focus of what we consider to be 'significant' in children's learning. These 'signifiers' of achievement, attainment and development of knowledge, skills, understanding and learning behaviours create a 'core' of that which practitioners are aware of and identify, and, as discussed, are viewed and perceived through a set of values and beliefs of what is considered to be 'important'. This in turn is strongly influenced by the curriculum or 'body of knowledge', culturally, historically and pragmatically defined, that we as a community consider to be important and necessary for children to acquire in order to be successful.

If we are to avoid a 'folk' model of assessment (Carr 2001), a model that is based on expediency and convenience, one that draws from an 'external' tradition, mythology and unfounded assumptions rather than accurate and authentic value-driven knowledge about children's learning, development and outcomes, then this will necessitate a brief overview of the two critical dimensions of 'signifiers'. It is important to note that the focus of this book is on children's Early Years, in this case defined as birth to 5 years, and, as such, the discussion will revolve around the specific needs and evidence for children of this age. One of the 'folklore' assumptions has been to treat Early Years children as a 'diluted version' of older children, and to replicate later expectations in a more simplified form. It is critical that this assumption is strongly and vigorously challenged by the weight of the evidence that surrounds it. Equally we need to ensure that as this is discussed it draws from and is influenced by the rich 'internal' traditions of early childhood education and the theories and philosophies which emanate from these, from the principle that Julie Fisher (2008) uses as the title of her book 'Starting *from* the child' (my emphasis).

Firstly, what do we know about the way young children learn and how their development in their Early Years is impacted by the provision, practice and pedagogy that they find themselves immersed in? As the primary purpose of assessment is specifically to support, enhance and challenge this process, understanding how this 'works' is of critical importance. We know more than ever about the manner in which children learn, therefore applying this to how it is recognised and assessed is of major importance.

Secondly, what do we know about what impacts most on young children's on-going development and later outcomes; what really matters to children and enables them to become successful? Which are the aspects, types and forms of learning – both in terms of content and learning behaviours – that most help children develop as learners and equip them with the necessary 'predications of success'? Conversely, what is less relevant or helpful for their long-term development? Is there evidence of anything that impacts in a particularly negative way and actually prevents the kind of outcomes we all want for our children, particularly in relation to the commonly held values identified in Chapter 2?

How do children learn?

Evangelou (2009, quoted in Tickell 2011) describes young children's learning and development as the interplay between 'interconnected and dynamic facets of the unique child with surrounding relationships and experiences' (2011: 23); children imitate and take cues and messages from the adults around them and process these to form learned cultural behaviours that define both the values and pragmatism of the surrounding community. Evangelou goes on to describe how 'value systems and beliefs mediate these ecological domains' (quoted in Tickell 2011: 86). Thus learning and development are, on the whole, not neutral 'inevitabilities', but the direct consequence of the interactions that children have with those around them and the environment they exist in, shaping their understanding and providing experiences and opportunities that consolidate and extend their learning. Underpinning this exist a range of necessary skills and behaviours that provide the context for such development to take place. All of which are, incidentally, 'learnable' behaviours and therefore teachable and assessable (Claxton 2004).

Developmental psychologists have identified aspects such as **self-regulation** and **metacognition** to be particularly important behaviours in defining and supporting the likelihood of on-going and later success in all domains.

Self-regulation is the ability to manage and control feeling and behaviours, to see beyond the immediate, and to have a wider understanding of how impulses and reactions impact on behaviour and possibilities.

Meta-cognition is the process of understanding and being aware of your own learning and being able to 'track back' and draw from knowledge and experiences to understand 'how' a concept or knowledge has been learned. The work of Carol Dweck (2006) on 'fixed and growth mindsets' identifies the critical role that **motivation** plays in applying and persisting with the development of skills and knowledge, the ability to overcome obstacles and the importance of persistence and resilience to achieving goals and outcomes; in other words to be successful. Additionally the work of Laevers and Declercq (2012) identify the importance of children's **'involvement'** in activity when children demonstrate the physical attributes of high-level concentration and preoccupation with, generally, a self-initiated activity. These indicators of 'high-level involvement' signify 'deep and significant' learning that connects directly with children's experiences and intrinsic motivations and establish important and authentic neurological connections. Leavers and Declercq (2012) also identify the importance of **well-being**, describing its presence as being apparent when the child is 'comfortable in their own skin' or 'like a fish in water', as a critical signifier of effective learning.

Vygotsky (1978) emphasised the importance of language in developing the child as a thinker and social being that can interact and relate to the environment and people around them. Language is critically related to thinking as it provides a connection between actions, thought and memory. Piaget described this as 'private speech' an on-going internal narrative with which we describe experiences and sensations, leading to the thoughts, speculations descriptions and hypotheses that follow them. Vygotsky also developed the theory of the 'Zone of Proximal Development' (ZPD) and talked of 'the distance between the actual developmental level as determined by independent problem solving and the level of potential development as determined through problem solving under adult guidance or collaboration with more capable peers' (Vygotsky 1978: 86). This is the 'gap' between what a child knows, understands and can do and the 'next step' in experience and/or learning and development. Vygotsky argues that in order to progress and develop, learners need a more experienced peer – or adult – to 'scaffold' and support this next phase of learning. The ZPD plays a critical role in assessment, particularly because it identifies the specific purpose of assessment – 'knowing and understanding the child' and also what is 'significant' for their on-going development – and the role of the adult in creating and enabling the next 'signifier' of the child's learning.

Loris Malaguzzi, whose philosophy underpins the world renowned pre-school system in Reggio Emilia in northern Italy, stressed the importance of community and belonging and the role of creativity. He identified key principles which define and create the ethos and purpose of education (http://www.sightlines-initiative.com):

• All children have potential

• Children are connected to their family, community, society, objects and symbols

• The reciprocity of children

• Children are communicators

• The environment is the third teacher

• Educators are partners, nurturers and guides

- Educators are researchers
- Documentation is important for communication
- Parents are partners
- Education is about asking questions.

Fisher (2008) acknowledges that while empirical evidence of how children learn is in short supply, it is still possible to identify the characteristics of this, and that these have been influential on the evolution of learning theories. She refers to the development of children's 'personal cognitive jigsaw' (2008: 28) in which attitudes, dispositions, skills, strategies and understandings (sometimes misunderstandings) are formed. The characteristics identified are that young children learn by:

- being active
- organising their own learning experiences
- using language
- interacting with others.

In her seminal and highly influential work *Early Childhood Education*, Bruce (1989) draws from the early childhood tradition and cites the 'common law' that unites the earliest pioneers (Frobel, Montessori and Steiner) in developing effective practice and provision for young children. From this, common principles are extrapolated that form the basis for understanding, supporting (and therefore assessing) young children's learning and development. She identifies these principles as:

1. Childhood is seen as valid in itself, as a part of life and not simply as a preparation for adulthood
2. The whole child is considered to be important
3. Learning is not compartmentalised, for everything links
4. Intrinsic motivation, resulting in child-initiated, self-directed activity is valued
5. Self-discipline is emphasised
6. There are specially receptive periods of learning at different stages of development
7. What children can do (rather than what they cannot do) is the starting point in the child's education

8. There is an inner life in the child which emerges especially under favourable conditions

9. The people (both adults and children) with whom the child interacts are of central importance

10. The child's education is seen as an interaction between the child and the environment the child is part of including, in particular, other people and knowledge itself. (Bruce 1989: 10)

What adds additional and compelling dimensions to the work of the Early Childhood theorists are the recent innovations and developments in the understanding of neuroscience and the development of its associated technology. The growth of non-invasive methods of reviewing, measuring and thus understanding brain activity has provided us with more scientifically based research into the complex workings of the human brain. More importantly, in this case, is what this can now suggest and assert in terms of how young children particularly retain, process and engage with learning, and how this both impacts on and is impacted by their specific phases of brain development. Interestingly, the tentative conclusions being drawn by neuroscientists would appear to back up and endorse the principles and philosophical starting points that the theorists of Early Education formulated with such visionary and intuitive accuracy.

Brain 'growth', the development and interconnection of dendrites and synapses, is the physical manifestation of learning and the impact of development. The 'density', that is, the number of such connections, and their strength, create the 'physical' framework within which learning takes place. Part of the significance of this is the change in our understanding of the impact of genetics and consequent dispositions which indicate that learning is a complex development that requires the interplay between a number of different factors. Knowledge in this area of science has radically challenged previous assumptions and 'truths' that have traditionally held sway.

This resonates strongly with the work of Dweck (2006) and her theory of 'mindset'. Dweck's research argues that the notion of 'intelligence' is not 'fixed' but 'growable' and that the development of a 'growth mindset' enables much greater chances of success.

The overwhelming significance here is the new belief, based on neuroscientific developments, that learning, far from being fixed and inherited is, as Claxton (2004) describes it, 'learnable' and that the most significant, 'fertile' phases of development occur specifically within the child's early years. In addition to this, there is clear evidence from both neurological and psychological standpoints that there are 'favourable conditions' for promoting learning and supporting development and that there are critical discussions to be had on the nature of how best to support – based on understanding and assessing – the learning and development that follows.

We may then conclude that there are key principles for understanding how learning and development is viewed, interpreted and therefore supported. To summarise, the key aspects underpinning effective learning are that children learn most effectively when they:

- Feel secure

- Can watch, imitate and be supported by the adults around them

- Have opportunities to develop their self-regulation and metacognition

- Have opportunities to process and understand multi-sensory experiences

- Are provided with cognitive and physical challenges, especially during self-initiated activities

- Are supported in order to articulate their own learning.

Bredekamp and Copple (1997) summarise the starting points for understanding the nature of children's development and considerations when identifying, reflecting and processing support, challenge and assessment. This provides the context in which we can begin to identify the significances and resultant 'signifiers' in children's learning and development.

- Development proceeds at varying rates from child to child as well as unevenly within different areas of children's functioning

- The domains of children's development – physical, social, emotional and cognitive – are closely related

- Development proceeds in predictable directions towards greater complexity, organisation and internalisation

- Play is an important vehicle for children's social, emotional and cognitive development

- Development advances when children have opportunities to practise new skills and they experience challenge just beyond their level of mastery

- Children demonstrate different modes of learning and different ways of representing what they know. (Bredekamp and Copple 1997)

What are the significant impacts on children's learning?

Within this broad framework of how children learn, we have discussed the critical dimensions, principles and the 'favourable conditions' for their successful development. It is important to now identify what the 'signifiers' for success could be. In a responsible and meaningful approach to assessment what is identified as 'significant' will need to link directly to that which we know is important, relevant and impactful on children's learning and outcomes, again within the context of declared values and aspirations. What is important at this juncture is to review the *evidence* of what this is or could be, rather than glibly fall into a set of uninformed assumptions and convenient faux 'measurements' of what is merely easy to measure, recalling the quote attributed to Einstein that 'not everything that can be counted, counts'. Children's learning is complex and idiosyncratic; it is unpredictable and at times seemingly unfathomable. If assessment is to be authentic and therefore meaningful and usable, then these 'signifiers' need to be driven by the evidence of what matters. The weight of empirical research into this area has grown and 'matured' over the last several years. I do not intend to provide an exhaustive overview of every study but have focused on the three that have been the most influential and significant in defining 'impactfulness'.

The Effective Provision of Pre-School Education (EPPE) project

The EPPE project is a longitudinal study of the long-term effects of pre-school experiences and pre-school education on a sample of 3000 English children. The research team has published findings on the effects of, amongst other aspects, pre-school provision on the children's intellectual, social and behavioural development at the ages of 4, 7, 11 and 14. The current conclusions from the research state that the benefits of a high quality pre-school experience persist through to the age of 14, and have an impact on outcomes for a range of curriculum subjects. The research also asserts that a high quality pre-school experience has a noticeably positive impact on pupil behaviour and self-regulation.

Within this extensive study, key aspects of pedagogy and consequent 'signifiers' of learning and development become apparent. The issue is one of ensuring a carefully defined 'high quality' pre-school setting and recognising the types of behaviours that children demonstrate in response to this, with its impact on later outcomes, as described above. The role of formative assessment within this is also strongly acknowledged: '… effective pedagogues assess children's performance to ensure the provision of challenging yet achievable experiences (i.e. within the ZPD) and provide formative feedback' (Siraj-Blatchford 2009).

Significance was also attached to the relationships between children and their importance within the pedagogical approaches that determined the setting. The study noted that: 'Effective settings view cognitive and social development as complementary and they support children in rationalising and talking through their conflicts' (Siraj-Blatchford 2009).

Another key feature of high quality identified was the practice of 'Sustained Shared Thinking' (SST). This was defined as: 'An episode in which two or more individuals "work together" in an intellectual way to solve a problem, clarify a concept, evaluate activities, extend a narrative etc. Both parties must contribute to the thinking and it must develop and extend' (Siraj-Blatchford 2009). In high quality provision there were significantly higher incidences of this taking place than in other qualities of provision.

The importance of developing and supporting children's metacognition was also identified as a key feature of high quality provision and was seen to play an important part in developing children's 'learning to learn' dispositions:

> The development of these sophisticated levels of abstraction (and metaconciousness) also facilitate the development of a wider metacognition. This metacognition required in learning to learn, also develops as the child finds it necessary to describe, explain and justify their thinking about different aspects of the world to others. (Siraj-Blatchford 2009)

Finally, the concept of 'playful pedagogy' is introduced as a key means to ensure quality of interaction, approach and therefore potential outcome; aspects of this were described as:

- Building on and extending the child's interests

- The child is usually physically, socially and intellectually active

- The learning is exploratory without necessarily fixed outcomes in mind

- Playful learning motivates children to try more challenging learning

- Children use, apply and extend their knowledge, skills and understanding through active exploration

- In social contexts children develop their capacities for cooperation and collaboration and can often explore complex ideas.

The HighScope Perry pre-school study

The HighScope Perry study is another highly influential longitudinal study that focused on the relative outcomes of a cohort of American children from deprived backgrounds attending different types of pre-school settings in the mid 1960s. As well as the 'control' group that did not attend a setting at all, different groups of children attended settings with different approaches to pedagogy. There was a marked difference between the children who attended the settings based on the HighScope principles (see below) and those who did not. The study followed children throughout their school years and into adulthood and discovered continuing lifelong correlations between the type of their pre-school experience and later outcomes.

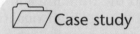 Case study

The HighScope Perry Preschool Project was evaluated in a randomized controlled trial of 123 children (58 were randomly assigned to a treatment group that received the program and a control group of 65 children that did not). Prior to the program, the preschool and control groups were equivalent in measures of intellectual performance and demographic characteristics. After the program the educational and life outcomes for the children receiving the program were much superior to outcomes for the children not receiving the program. The effects were significant ....

Educational outcomes for preschool group (versus control group):

At age 27 follow-up

- Completed an average of almost 1 full year more of schooling (11.9 years vs. 11 years)

- Spent an average of 1.3 fewer years in special education services – e.g., for mental, emotional, speech, or learning impairment (3.9 years vs. 5.2 years)

- 44 percent higher high school graduation rate (66% vs. 45%)

Pregnancy outcomes for preschool group (versus control group):

At age 27 follow-up

- Much lower proportion of out-of-wedlock births (57% vs. 83%)

- Fewer teen pregnancies on average (0.6 pregnancies/woman vs. 1.2 pregnancies/woman)

Lifetime criminal activity for preschool group (versus control group):

At age 40 follow-up

- 46 percent less likely to have served time in jail or prison (28% vs. 52%)
- 33 percent lower arrest rate for violent crimes (32% vs. 48%)

Economic outcomes for preschool group (versus control group):

At age 40 follow-up

- 42 percent higher median monthly income ($1,856 vs. $1,308)
- 26 percent less likely to have received government assistance (e.g. welfare, food stamps) in the past ten years (59% vs. 80%)

The relevant and appropriate central concepts and principles behind what is described as the High/Scope approach is as follows:

Active learning

The HighScope Curriculum emphasizes active participatory learning. Active learning means students have direct, hands-on experiences with people, objects, events, and ideas. Children's interests and choices are at the heart of the HighScope programs. They construct their own knowledge through interactions with the world and the people around them. In active learning settings, adults expand children's thinking with diverse materials and nurturing interactions.

Learning environment

A HighScope school classroom is divided into well-defined interest areas that typically include a house area, art area, block area, toy area, and other areas that reflect the children's interests. Children are able to access all facilities independently as well as take some responsibility for use of these areas.

Daily routine

HighScope classrooms follow a predictable sequence of events called the daily routine. The daily routine in a HighScope classroom includes plan-do-review, small- and large-group times, outside time, transition times, and eating and resting times.[1][non-primary source needed ....

Plan-do-review

A key component of the HighScope approach is the plan-do-review sequence. Children first plan what materials they want to work with, what they want to do, and whom they want to do it with (this can be done formally or informally in small groups). Once they have made a plan, however vague, of what they want to do, they can go and do it. Then, after this chosen worktime, the children discuss what they did and whether it was the same as, or different from, what they had planned.

Continues

Continued

Adult-child interaction

Shared control between adults and children is central to the HighScope Curriculum. In addition to sharing control, adults in a HighScope classroom participate in children's play, converse as partners with them, focus on children's strengths and offer them support, and encourage children's problem solving ....

Key developmental indicators

The HighScope Curriculum is organized into eight content areas: (1) approaches to learning; (2) language, literacy, and communication; (3) social and emotional development; (4) physical development and health; (5) mathematics; (6) science and technology; (7) social studies; and (8) creative arts. Within these content areas are 58 key developmental indicators (KDIs). The KDIs are statements of observable behaviors that define the important learning areas for young children. HighScope teachers keep these indicators in mind when they set up the learning environment and plan activities ....

Assessment

HighScope assesses children's development with comprehensive observations. HighScope teachers record daily anecdotes describing what children do and say. Several times a year, teachers review these anecdotes and rate each child using an assessment tool that is organized into six areas of development. These scores help the teachers design developmentally appropriate learning opportunities and can be used to explain children's progress during conferences.

Conflict Resution

HighScope has a six-step process that can be used to help children resolve conflicts that may arise during their day.

(Hohmann et al. 2008)

Rebecca Marcon: 'Moving up the Grades: Relationship between Preschool Model and Later School Success'

The American Developmental Psychologist Rebecca Marcon conducted a follow-up study on a group of children as they progressed through the educational process. She focused on the 'type' of pre-school provision the children had experienced and in particular the pedagogical 'models' used in the pre-schools they attended. These models were scrutinised according to learning experiences based on:

1. Scope of developmental goals

2. Conception of how children learn

3. Amount of autonomy given to the child

4. Conception of teacher's role

5. Provision of possibilities for learning from peers. (Marcon 2002)

This then led to the classification of the pedagogical models into one of three types:

- Child Initiated (CI) which were 'composed of child development-oriented teachers who facilitated learning by allowing children to actively direct the focus of their learning' (Marcon 2002)

- Academically Directed (AD) which 'represented more academically oriented teachers who preferred more direct instruction and teacher-directed learning experiences for pre-schoolers' (Marcon 2002)

- Middle of the Road (M) 'represented teachers whose beliefs and practices fell in between the other two opposing models by endorsing a combination approach.

Her conclusion was that:

> By the end of children's fifth year in school, there were no significant differences in academic performance of children who had experienced three different preschool models. By the end of their sixth year in school, children whose preschool experiences had been academically directed earned significantly lower grades compared to children who had attended child-initiated preschool classes. Children's later school success appears to have been enhanced by more active, child-initiated early learning experiences. Their progress may have been slowed by overly academic preschool experiences that introduced formalized learning experiences too early for most children's developmental status. (Marcon 2002)

Providing some historical context to the concerns being investigated, Marcon also noted that:

> Beginning in the 1980s, leading early childhood experts expressed concern about the wisdom of overly didactic, formal instructional practices for young children (e.g., Elkind, 1986; Zigler, 1987). They feared that short-term academic gains would be offset by long-term stifling of children's motivation and self-initiated learning. Later research suggests that these early concerns were warranted. Compared to children whose kindergarten experience emphasized child-initiated learning, primary-grade teachers rated children from didactic, teacher-centered kindergartens lower in conduct and work-study habits, and perceived them to be more distractible, less willing to follow directions, and less prosocial (Hart, Charlesworth, Burts, & DeWolf, 1993). Stipek, Feiler, Daniels, and Milburn (1995) also found motivational differences favoring a child-initiated view of early education compared to a more formalized, didactic approach. They cautioned that early academic gains in reading skills associated with didactic instruction of preschoolers 'come with some costs' that could have long-term negative effects on achievement. (Marcon 2002)

The reason that Marcon's work is of such interest, and of such significance when considering the approaches to assessment, is that, as
discussed in previous chapters, there is often a pressure – generally
externally driven – to focus on the didactic teaching of content in a formalised manner. Partly this is in order to fulfil politically motivated
targets, and partly this is because the 'regurgitation' of content, facts
and superficial skills is much simpler to assess, measure and 'numericalise'; if we recall Säljö's (1979) five categories of learning then this
kind of approach focuses on the first three at the exclusion of the final
two. The key concern here, is that, considering what the studies cited
allude to, this does not support the aspects and dimensions of children's learning that *matter* and are signifiers of the potential for later
success; they are then detached from the more significant aspects of
what might be termed 'learning behaviours'. Equally, the finding that
purely academic outcomes themselves are negatively affected by the
pedagogical model that focuses on content detached from context, is a
highly important aspect for consideration.

Therefore, in addressing the two questions, how do children learn
and what are the significant impacts on children's learning, we have
initiated the beginnings of what should underpin developing an
approach to meaningful, purposeful assessment. What we assess
reflects what we teach, provide for and value, so this starting point
will inevitably be immersed in a view and understanding of pedagogy. By reviewing the theories and evidence of what matters and
what has an impact, we have clear starting points and a broad
consensus on identifying the significant behaviours and signifiers
that should form the basis of assessment and shape the key
considerations when assessing young children.

There is a broad agreement that children's learning is a unique, individualised process and that each trajectory and journey of development
will contain different, contradictory, diverse and idiosyncratic dimensions and episodes. There is no template for this and effective
assessment needs to acknowledge that as we begin to understand and
make judgements on children's learning and development this will
vary considerably from child to child. As well as the difference in these
'journeys' there will also be a critical difference in the way that children
demonstrate these 'signifiers', and effective assessment will rely on the
ability of the practitioner to see beyond the immediate 'product' into
the thinking, behaviours and significances that lie beneath it.

There is an acknowledgment too, that the role of 'active learning';
hands-on, practical application rather than abstract detachment; is of
vital importance to authentic assessment. The role of play, self-initiated

activity, is a vital means by which children demonstrate what they truly know and understand; because in this 'locus of control' at their highest levels of motivation, children will draw together everything, cognitively, physically, academically and socially to converge on the moment in time when a challenge, problem or expression drives their energy and desire. So again, for assessment to be effective and 'real', the skill of the practitioner will be required to enable this to flourish, through the decisions they make in terms of interaction, support, intervention and challenge and the ways in which the environment enables and establishes the conditions for children to express and demonstrate learning at this high self-motivated level.

Underpinning all of these aspects is the critical notion of 'well-being', the sense of feeling secure, unthreatened and being as Laevers and Declercq state, 'like a fish in water' (Laevers and Declercq 2012). Children in this state are more able to demonstrate the critical 'risks' in behaviour and learning on which brain growth is dependent; therefore an awareness – an assessment or knowledge – of their levels and types of well-being is critical for setting the foundations for effective and sustained development.

Equally critical for development is the use of language in terms of communicating with adults and peers but also in linking thought, knowledge and memory and constructing children's identity as learners (Carr and Lee 2012).

What also appears to emerge from the review of children's learning and what is significant is the primary role of 'learning behaviours' as the key signifiers and indicators of effective development and predictors of more favourable long-term sustained outcomes. There is a strong focus on the need for the qualities and traits of self-regulation and self-organisation as pre-requisites for effective learning. Although these are clearly developmentally visible in children of all ages, and therefore assessable, it is contestable whether or not these are aspects that are measureable in any real sense. Practitioners' understanding and knowledge in an 'informed intuitive' sense are more substantially relied on to identify and support these critical skills. Again, pressure to 'numericalise' this needs to be resisted, and it also has to be defended as a critical aspect of learning even if such measurement is not possible.

Equally there is a strong agreed emphasis on the importance of developing children's metacognition and the ability to reflect on and examine their own thinking and thought processes. Evidence from a range of the sources cited above indicates that this is a significant cognitive development strongly linked to both 'quality' of experience and long-term outcomes. Aligned to this are Dweck's (2006, 2012) theory of 'fixed and growth mindset' and the EPPE project's (Sylva et al. 2010) description of the importance of episodes of 'Sustained Shared Thinking'. These features of development and high-level approaches to thinking and developing cognitive strength are vital in understanding both the nature of children and supporting their on-going development and possibilities as learners. Again, as this is a vital part of significant impactful learning, it needs to be considered as a critical component of assessment. Any kind of 'measurement' for this, or strict and strictly enforced criterion will undoubtedly undermine its very purpose or potential impact. Much of these behaviours or signifiers depend on the notion of a child's intrinsic motivation, persistence, tenacity, risk taking and responding to challenge. Equally, children's demonstrated level of involvement, engagement, 'intensity' of concentration in an activity or moment need to be identified as key signifiers of learning. It is important to also recognise that these are learned and learnable behaviours, and that they thrive in environments and contexts which acknowledge them and their importance. Again, these form a basis to an underlying pedagogy and, although not 'taught' in a formalised sense, will be supported, modelled and demonstrated by practitioners. Their *significance* is in identifying and supporting learning through a descriptive, qualitative and relative approach, and again care should be taken not to formalise or attempt to 'measure' this in any overly clinical mathematical manner.

The evidence, particularly from the EPPE research, also identified the importance of self-managed (though supported) conflict resolution as a key signifier for success. The role of social interaction and cooperation has long been identified by developmental psychologists as a key feature of effective learning and a prerequisite for both individual and group success (Whitebread 2012). The notion of how children engage with this and manage differences and points of disagreement forms the basis of critical lifelong human skills and ability.

Finally, although these 'learning behaviours' have been identified as the key 'signifiers' of learning and development, both significant and assessable, it is important to recognise that they do not exist in a context-free space. The content – the body of knowledge sometimes referred to as 'curriculum content' – also plays a key role. As I have previously discussed, the nature and content of this is both value driven and culturally and historically determined and exists as a key factor in equipping children with the information required to exist and be successful in the world. What is important at this juncture, given the evidence and discussion above, is that the 'fact based' content does not override the learning behaviours that it context-ualises. Marcon's work is particularly relevant in highlighting the negative impact of an overly academic/content pedagogy, while the EPPE project is equally focused on the importance of learning behaviours. This is not to state that the content is irrelevant – far from it – but it is to acknowledge that however easy 'fact regur-gitation' is to measure, it is not what is truly significant for children's learning and developmental success.

 Reflective task

Observing the children you work with as a practitioner, what are the aspects of their learning, development and behaviour that you identify as the most significant and important?

Further reading

Marsden, L. and Woodbridge, J. (2005) *Looking Closely at Learning and Teaching … A Journey of Development.* Huddersfield: Early Excellence.
Laevers, F. and Declercq, B. (eds) (2012) *A Process-Orientated Monitoring System for the Early Years (POMS).* CEGO.
Stewart, N. (2011) *How Children Learn: The Characteristics of Effective Early Learning.* London: Early Education.

5

The Intuitive Professional

This chapter will:
- Identify the key aspects of effective practitioner behaviours
- Clarify how decisions are made by practitioners and how this impacts on the approach to pedagogy, interaction and assessment
- Reassert the importance of informed professional judgement and explore the external pressures on this

In the first chapter of this book I briefly mentioned the nature, role and motivations of the Early Years practitioner and the impact this has on the children they work with and the future society that forms as a result. In this chapter I would like to further explore the nature of this role and the issues, considerations and challenges that Early Years practitioners face in delivering effective and principled pedagogy in the settings where they work. Turning specifically to the context of approaches to assessment, I intend to identify key principles and considerations in negotiating, accommodating and utilising both the external pressures and the internal aspirations that practitioners engage with on a daily basis as part of their role.

When we take the decision to become an Early Years practitioner, we decide that we will spend our professional lives thinking about and interacting with young children, delighting in the significant part of their lives that they spend with us, and celebrating their developments, achievements, fascinations, ideas and uniqueness. As practitioners we realise that we change children's lives and possibilities thorough the conversations we have with them, the opportunities and experiences we make available to them and the approaches we take that empower them as thinkers, learners and doers. Because we know that children learn through watching and imitating the adults around them, our role as a significant presence in their lives has a dramatic impact on how they develop their perceptions and understanding of the world around them. Equally, we are all too aware that each decision we take opens or closes possibilities and that our responsibility to take them into the unknown is a keenly felt and potent one.

So when we decide do this, a complex set of psychological, social, philosophical and emotional forces combine to impact on that decision. In becoming Early Years practitioners, many of us draw from our own early childhood experiences as an inspiration that shapes the rationale for this decision and the subsequent approaches that we take and the ethos and philosophies that we embrace. Sometimes this evolves from positive experiences that we want to recreate and replicate, passing on this positivity to forthcoming generations so they too can benefit from similar experiences. Yet sometimes this decision emanates from negative experiences that we want to 'reclaim' and 'redeem' for children that we work with so that their experience will be a different and more positive one – the 'teaching by default' or counter-narrative that is positive by implicit contradiction.

In either case, or in a multitude of variations between them, we take that decision starting with dual points of reference and motivation. These have been referred to as 'socially just and child-centred practices' (Rose and Rogers 2012).

Socially just and child-centred practice

The idea of 'socially just practice' emanates from a set of beliefs – the 'value prism' through which we view the world that I have referred to earlier – and defines what we think and believe to be important. This influences our approaches, understanding and interpretations of what we see, as well as the decisions that we take. Although it could be argued that these are 'subconscious' rather than overt influences, they are nevertheless a very powerful aspect of the decision making process.

Alongside this, the notion of 'child-centred practice', '... viewing the child as intrinsically curious and capable, respecting children's rights as well as their needs and interests, and a commitment to active learning and free play' (Rose and Rogers 2012: 6), is also strongly influential. This often revolves around an intuitive trait of being able to communicate with children, follow their interests and respect the very individuality and idiosyncrasy that other adults who are not Early Years practitioners find so daunting, bewildering and frustrating. As practitioners, we revel in this apparent chaos of learning and through it find the 'invisible moments of possibility' within which we extend and develop the child as a learner, with the idea of significances and signifiers strongly at the forefront of our thinking. However, part of the delight of working with young children and the motivation that sustains us is precisely the unexpected perceptions, the pure originality, natural surrealism and unpredictable connections that children make and share with us; 'unfettered' by the logical and rational templates of reality that we form through experience, children's view of themselves and the world they live in is 'unique 'in the truest meaning of the word. It is important to be aware of the nature of this at our particular juncture in this book as these intuitions form a critical aspect of Early Years pedagogy, and are highly potent in how we ensure that practice and provision are as effective as possible; although it may appear to be a simple and straightforward approach, it is littered with potential obstacles and complications – and, given the pressures, mythologies and folklores eluded to, no more obviously than in the area of assessment.

Effective practitioner behaviours

It is also important to be aware of, explore and reassert the critical importance that practitioners have, especially in Early Years settings, on children's learning and development, and how the decisions they take, daily and constantly, impact on the learning process.

The EPPE study (Sylva et al. 2010), as discussed in Chapter 4, sustained a long-term view of the impact of pre-school provision on children at ages, 7, 11 and 14, and was particularly concerned with the variations that occurred in relation to the *quality* of provision that the child accessed. The study's conclusion was that quality was a critical factor in the long-term impact of the provision and therefore needed to be defined and explored carefully and rigorously. As a result of this the study identified five specific areas within the realm of pedagogy that it concluded were particularly important and related to longer-term impact. These were:

• Quality of the adult–child verbal interaction

- Knowledge and understanding of the curriculum
- Knowledge of how young children learn
- Adults' skill in supporting children in resolving conflicts
- Helping parents to support children's learning at home. (Sylva et al. 2010)

In an additional dimension to the study, the project focused on exploring the difference between Early Years settings that achieved 'good' compared to 'excellent' outcomes. It is important to point out that the definition of 'outcomes' covered a broader range of learning and developmental behaviours than what could be defined as narrow 'curricular' outcomes. These were seen to be pivotal in the potential for on-going and later success. The study focused on the percentage of time children were engaged in 'high cognitive challenge', similar to the aspect that Laevers and Declercq (2012) describe as 'high levels of involvement' and the 'initiation category' – these being either child-initiated or adult-directed in nature. Through this study it became apparent that the significant difference between the relative success of the settings was difference in the amount of time children spent having their self-initiated activity subsequently supported by an adult. This critical distinction rests entirely on the skill and judgement of the adult practitioner in when to observe and when to intervene and interact, as well as in the nature of that interaction and the level of understanding that is brought to that moment. As discussed in previous chapters, these 'moments of invisible possibility', critical to children's learning, sometimes momentary and fragile, often precarious and finely balanced, result from the decision that practitioners take, in the micro-moment, framed within their knowledge of the significance and signifiers of children's learning and their understanding of what is possible, desirable and necessary for children to develop. The delicate and considered approach to this which practitioners take is vital in establishing the significant 'learning behaviours' discussed in Chapter 4, children's 'ownership' of their own learning and their self-perception as effective and competent learners.

The impact of this should never be underestimated. Tina Bruce (1999: 34) notes that:

> The appreciation that young children feel for the rest of their lives towards those who have contributed in a major way to how they feel about themselves as learners is rarely spoken. It is an abstract intuitive thing which they take with them through their lives. And yet, it anchors them forever, and it is sometimes called having a sense of well-being.

So the impact of the role is a critical one, as the decisions taken affect the future of children's successful development in a range of 'spoken and unspoken ways'. As previously discussed, much of young children's learning is imitative in nature, therefore the impact of the adult has equal weighting on teaching children 'how to be' in terms of their own traits, propensities and actions. Evidently the role of the Early Years practitioner is both a highly complex and highly intricate one.

In their exploration of the role of the adult, Rose and Rogers (2012) make reference to the 'plural practitioner', which consists of 'seven selves' of characteristics that each 'blend into and help to create the next'. One of these 'selves' is, of course; 'The Assessor' and another, equally significant in this chapter, is that of 'The Critical Reflector' (Rose and Rogers 2012: 3). This is the first characteristic to be explored, deliberately to 'communicate its significance' (2012: 13), and it is described as the way in which 'practitioners' values, beliefs, attitudes, knowledge, and assumptions about young children directly affect the provision they seek to create and the nature of their interactions with children' (2012: 13).

This notion of critical reflection, both of in terms of practitioners' own practice, and more crucially the external pressures that might be perceived to be apparently very powerful and overwhelming, is an essential element of this role and particularly relevant to the area of assessment. As decisions get taken practitioners process information with which to take further decisions about interaction, observation and provision, culminating possibly in assertions, judgements or conclusions in the realm of accountability. These decisions will most certainly drive actions and activity in supporting significances or signifiers as developments in learning. In this context, an element of reflection – passing this information unadulterated and undiluted through the 'value prism' to ensure that the decision is an effective and appropriate one – becomes ever more critical. There can easily be a tendency to be swayed, distracted or affected by the real or perceived external pressures and expectations – a conscious or subconscious attempt at 'second guessing' what is 'supposed to happen'. But with the critical nature of interaction lying at the heart of these decisions, if the net result of this is being compromised, then the moment in children's learning so dependent on it can become lost. The intuitive decisions, and informed reactions to signifiers and significances, can be a casualty to the demands – perceived or real – of external expectations and assumptions.

In Kathleen Gooch's intense study of the nature, skills and traits of two Early Years practitioners (Gooch 2010) she identifies 'defining elements of practice' that present the effectiveness that certainly strives 'towards excellence' as the title of her book suggests.

One of these defining elements is what she describes as 'wittingness', for which she draws on the work of Peters (1966). She describes this in the context of the practitioner's responsibility and the necessity for them to be 'conscious of their actions' (1966: 128) and to act 'intentionally' in all aspects of their work in supporting children's learning. What she then proceeds to describe as 'witting' practitioners carefully design all aspects of possibility – both overt and 'incidental' – and create the environment in which learning behaviours, discovered through emulation and proactive 'intentional' support, can thrive.

Again, this is critically intuitive pedagogical behaviour, of which assessment, knowledge and understanding of the children is a key part; it is not a 'formula' in any way nor reliant on a conscious consideration of external expectation, ratio of time and approach or prescribed action. A necessarily important aspect of this is identifying significances and signifiers, which lies at the central point of effective, principled and responsible practice. As the culmination of a range of knowledges and understandings and as an awareness of the impact of each decision and action, practitioners need to demonstrate and rely on this 'wittingness' to ensure that these decisions remain undiluted.

Part of this decision making also rests with the 'types' of interactions and activities that practitioners engage in; how their knowledge of the individual child and the signifiers of development are approached. There is often much debate about the necessary 'balance' of child-initiated and adult-directed activities that children should experience, and often a perception amongst practitioners that there is a set formula, ratio or percentage of time that children should spend between them. Julie Fisher (2008) identifies the three 'types' and their 'concerns' in terms of pedagogy. These are:

• Adult focused as the 'intended learning'

• Adult-directed as 'potential learning' and

• Child initiated as 'spontaneous learning'.

What needs to be considered here is not an artificial formula between these but the understanding of how the interplay between these 'different types' of practitioner activity work together and are at the disposal of the adult to refine and adapt as the moment dictates. Again, this rests with values, decisions and the self-confidence in the pedagogy and approach being used. Any consideration of a perceived formula or time percentage will only compromise this moment and negatively impact on the intuition and 'wittingness' of the practitioner.

In their exploration and explanation of the Early Excellence approach to effective Early Years practice, provision and pedagogy, Marsden and Woodbridge (2005) identify the role of the adult as a key element or 'corner' of the pedagogical model, and the most significant aspect of this as 'the skilful ... way in which we scaffold children's learning. We provide the bridge between what children already know and understand, and what they will learn next given attentive guidance and support' (2005: 9). This is further identified as to critical aspects of support:

1. 'Responding to the learner' ... By responding to children and to their ideas, thoughts and feelings, educators promote a string sense of well-being, creating the safety within which children can push at the boundaries of what they already know and understand. (Marsden and Woodbridge 2005: 9)

2. 'Contributing to the learning' Our commitment to children as strong powerful learners ... informs our understanding that chil dren come to learn about their world through discovery rather than by being told about it. But children also need new information and fresh experiences that promote further learning. (Marsden and Woodbridge 2005: 9)

The EPPE study (Sylva et al. 2010) also identifies significant pedagogical behaviours that are considered to impact on the outcomes and quality of pre-school provision with the implications and consequences that have been alluded to above.

The study identifies key principles of effective early pedagogy and a range of behaviours:

> ... effective pedagogues model appropriate language, values and practices, encourage socio-dramatic play, praise, encourage, ask questions, and interact verbally with children. Excellent settings tended to achieve an equal balance between teacher-led and child-initiated interactions, play and activities. (Siraj-Blatchford 2009)

One of these significant behaviours is teachers' extending activities:

> ... a particular form of teacher initiation that may also be applied in cases where initially the child initiated. The most effective settings were found to provide both teacher-initiated group work and freely chosen yet potentially instructive play activities. 'Extension' was included in the definition of 'sustained shared thinking. (Siraj-Blatchford 2009)

Then, perhaps most critically, they identify the importance of differentiation and assessment: '... effective pedagogues assess children's performance to ensure the provision of challenging yet achievable experiences (i.e. within the ZPD) and provide formative feedback' (Siraj-Blatchford 2009).

The explicit purpose of assessment is to ascertain the point on development, the propensity for extension, the skill, knowledge, understanding and/or motivation to be built on by the practitioner. It therefore follows that of all the continual decisions that practitioners take, those related specifically or more broadly around this become the most important and influential in the child's learning. The expression of values, through identifying significances and signifiers in moments or extended episodes of children's activity, whether adult led, adult initiated or child initiated, forms the basis of how pedagogy is articulated and communicated, whether overtly or implicitly. Rose and Rogers (2012) argue that assessment is essentially about 'making a value judgement' (2003: 113) and that this is ultimately an expression of power over children. However, it is an inevitable reality that children attend settings with practitioners who have their own beliefs and knowledges, with expectations and aspirations that manifest themselves out of these, with resources that the adults have selected, routines and expectations that have been declared, and therefore assessments are made that reflect this. If we take a definition of assessment as much more than simply making a value judgement, as one would in a criterion referenced or standardised assessment (see Chapter 3), and if we define it as the 'knowing and understanding of children' and are acutely aware of what is significant and what we consider to be important – the inevitable consequences and foundations of any pedagogy – then assessment is not a power *over* children but the critical means to an empowering *of* children as learners. If we consider how this ties in with a sensitive, developmentally appropriate pedagogy that understands the significance of learning behaviours that can be meaningfully contextualised by content and the agreed 'bodies of knowledge' and the range of strategies and attributes identified by EPPE as being particularly impactful and significant, then how practitioners take decisions within the realm of this assessment becomes all the more potent and precious.

The issue of balance within how practitioners teach is reflected inevitably in the realm of assessment. Again, decisions taken by practitioners, particularly momentary ones in the context of interactions, subtly and sometimes more overtly shape both the learning possibility but also the knowledge and understanding – significances and signifiers – that can be demonstrated by the child. The kinds of considerations identified by Rose and Rogers (2012) are typical of those everyday reflective questions that practitioners ask themselves as children's activity and learning behaviours emerge in front of them:

- At what point should I intervene?

- What level and kind of support is appropriate?

- When does intervention become interference?

- What kinds of questions are appropriate?

- When do I tell them the right answer or help them?

- Will my intervention stop it from being child-led?

- Does child-led mean the same thing as child-initiated? (Rose and Rogers 2012: 7)

Critical again is the understanding and acknowledgement that opportunities to self-initiate, to engage in self-motivated play, provide the optimum theatre for the most accurate and authentic demonstrations of knowledge, skills and understanding. This is not merely a function of an assessment process but vital for children to 'make sense' of their learning and therefore demonstrate its meaning and purpose for them. Laevers' work on involvement (see Chapter 4) describes this as the 'flow and high energy level' that children exhibit when learning is at its most significant, profound and determined. Without the opportunity to self-initiate, not only will the 'knowing and understanding' of the child be severely limited to that which the adult requests, but it will be decontextualised and separate from what is meaningful for the child. Ultimately it becomes surface level rather than significant learning, as Bruce (1999) notes while considering the over-structured lives of some children's home and school experience:

> These children have no time to be anchored enough or to be able to think and feel, to relate to others clearly, for play helps children to unravel their lives and experiences in ways which hold meaning for them. An over taught, over structured life, means that there is no time for children to apply and use what they have learnt for play is primarily about the application of what has been learnt and helps children to sort out understanding. (Bruce 1999: 39)

This perhaps is another difference between *'power over'* children and *'empowering'* children as learners. The skills that matter, that make most difference, are those that incorporate the traits, attributes and intuitions that inspire and motivate practitioners in the first place. Ann Clare (2012), writing specifically about practitioners working with children aged from birth to 3 sums up the essence of what this involves:

The best practitioners are those who follow the children's lead and who are genuinely involved. Young children are perceptive and know when an adult is 'faking' their enjoyment. A good early years practitioner is one who does not have to speak all the time, and can sit and play alongside children in quiet reflection. (Clare 2012: 35)

So throughout any examinations of effective pedagogical app-roaches, the way in which practitioners make decisions, particularly in the areas of 'momentary interaction', is a critical part of their role. In these moments when actions or inactions are decided, practi-tioners shape both learning opportunities for children and gleaning the appropriate information – in other words making assessments – on which those decisions are based. As I have explored already, these are driven through values and beliefs; knowledges and the identification of significances that we decide it is important for children to know, understand and be able to do. This process of 'filtering' perceptions and 'importances' is an inevitable one, and critically reflective practitioners will be aware of how this impacts on their day-to-day practice and particularly their interactions with children. Practitioners will also be aware that each decision they take will be laced with importance and impact directly on the children that they work with.

Professional judgement

What should be crucially apparent throughout every stage of this decision making process is the practitioners' own professional judgement regarding the nature and conclusion of each of those decisions.

Part of this is built upon the information we glean from reading, our initial training, on-going professional development, our own informal action research and the results of wider, more compre-hensive research studies such as the EPPE project. As reflective practitioners, keen to be effective – the best we can be – a process of reconstructing, reaffirming and challenging this knowledge is continually taking place.

The other part is drawing upon the skills, traits and propensities I referred to at the beginning of this chapter, those that stem naturally from the rationale of deciding to become an Early Years practitioner and devote our professional life to working with and for young children. Rose and Rogers (2012) refer to the notion of 'intuitive theories' which interact with the information being processed about the role and combine with personal values, beliefs and our view and perceptions of children, their learning and development. As this develops and modifies itself in the light of new information, new ideas and the sustained momentum of experience, it forms a tangible and embedded 'personal pedagogy' that we take with us as both our starting point and touchstone to all aspects of our role as a practitioner.

This professionalism, based on 'informed intuition' and the reflective process that enhances and develops our practice, rests on our confidence to trust and support it, acknowledging our own expertise and being ready and able to articulate its defence when necessary.

A typical practitioner takes many, many, life changing decisions every day – sometimes overt and dramatic, most of the time subtle and 'under the surface' and often, particularly through long experience, without overt consciousness. This could be the way we talk to a child – the carefully considered and pitched language we use and the stimulation this provides – or this could be how we suggest an idea or create and maintain a warm caring ethos and environment in which the kinds of learning outcomes we aspire to have the opportunity to take root and thrive. The important consideration at this point is that during these decisions a 'pure' informed view of what matters, what we consider to be important and what we know affects the learning and development of children, is the main driver for how that decision is considered and taken.

There are no rigid, clinical or forensic templates for effective and successful pedagogy, no formulas or lists of activities that if completed create good outcomes for learning and development. There is no 'holy grail' of specific prescribed actions that result in what we want for children, as through their uniqueness of experiences, propensities and nature they defy any single categorisation of a one size homogenous fit. What does exist are the values and beliefs we have as practitioners, the principles we operate by and our knowledge – our 'informed intuition' that enables us to support and adapt to the children we work with. The role of assessment – the knowing and understanding of children – plays the most critical part in this as it forms the decisions we take and the consequent shape and direction that children's 'life journeys' then take.

The reason that this is so pertinent is that there is often a tendency for practitioners to fall into what might be termed 'compliance anxiety'. This can often manifest itself in a concern of practitioners that they are 'doing the right thing' – not necessarily for the children that they work with but in terms of external demands and pressures that have set up a particular expectation of what should and shouldn't be done. Worse still, this 'compliance anxiety' becomes so powerful in the mind of the practitioner that it can culminate in actions and approaches that compromise their principles, values and 'informed intuition' in order to meet an external requirement or second guess what a perceived expectation might be.

In addition to this, the situation is sometimes compounded by the added phenomenon of 'format dependency', as though there is a specific pro-forma or document that if completed in a certain way will be the answer to and panacea for effective pedagogy. Practitioners are often known to spend large amounts of time completing such paperwork, or electronic submissions – not because it will help them know children better, understand them more thoroughly or inform their approach to pedagogy, but because an external expectation has deemed it to be a necessary requirement.

Gooch (2010) refers to Brown (2003) who discusses the 'cultures of insiders and outsiders', claiming that 'outsiders', who are defined as 'prescriptive policy makers', often prescribe the practice for 'insiders'. The discussion then concludes that: 'if innovation for improvement is to be effective it has to be rooted in … the ways in which the insiders make sense of what they do and these do not necessarily reflect the conceptual frameworks used by insiders' (Gooch 2010: 135).

It is quite clear, in the current context of Early Years practitioners, where the power in this dynamic lies and where it should lie. As the 'insiders' working day to day with the reality of children, practitioners often feel pressured by the demands of the 'outsiders' wanting the complexity of children's development and learning to be reduced to a simplistic formula, preferably numerical, that will justify and be accountable for short-term political credit. Although the rationale behind this may have been originally an honourable and reasonable – even principled – one that aims to secure the best for children, by the time it impacts 'on the ground' such uninformed simplicity can have the opposite impact.

In the arena of assessment this often leads to expedient, irrelevant and misguided attempts to meet the demands of the 'outsiders', even if this compromises what we know to be effective and based on significances and signifiers and the intuitive knowledge of children. Often, ideas are embraced and followed with the necessary understanding or the belief that they reflect the practitioner's own values and approaches. Most frequently, this occurs within the area of record keeping and documentation, which will be explored in more detail in Chapter 7. Often a format is 'delivered' to settings and there is an expectation that it is used by everyone. Compliance anxiety is triggered and all practitioners wholeheartedly use what has been given to them. The syndrome of 'format dependency' has now been fatefully secured. However, because it is not 'owned' by the practitioners, because they are not aware of the process by which it was developed, it becomes merely 'something to be done' without purpose or real meaning. In the very worst cases, approaches to documentation and recording, based on good intentions and effective assessment but imposed on practitioners, become a distraction from supporting learning and development and an unwelcome additional tier of, at best, unnecessary and, at worst, damaging bureaucracy.

Because what practitioners do is so important, because it impacts so forcefully on children's lives, potentials and possibilities, it is critical that a strong, confident, informed path is cut through this and that practitioners maintain a 'laser beam' focus on what is right for children, eschewing a dependency on external demands where they conflict with or compromise the principles of effective pedagogy. As previously discussed, accountability for the actions of practitioners is an important element of what is done, but this has to be *owned* by the practitioner themselves and has to be *real* in terms of what is significant and important. Any principled and respectful 'outsider' would acknowledge this and build their own measures, descriptions and approaches to accountability around the practitioner, rather than impose something alien and pointless without any regard for the professionalism and knowledge that is already firmly in situ.

It might be argued that this position is an unrealistic one and doesn't take account of the environment in which settings exist and the reasonable expectations of accountability. However, it is worth considering that we all have a 'personalised construction of reality' (Rose and Rogers 2012: 19) and that to a greater or lesser extent we choose what realities we accept and those which we challenge. For example, we cannot successfully challenge and dismiss the law of gravity or the fact that we need food, water and air to survive. We have only a limited and occasional opportunity to challenge the reality of government policy, media pronouncements on the effectiveness of practitioners and employers' approaches to remuneration.

However, there are day-to-day realities that we can challenge and construct ourselves because the locus of power exists with the practitioner. We can reclaim what we know is important and right for children and challenge any attempts to distract, compromise or interfere with this. Through our expertise, our knowledge, the value prism and the intuition that makes us as skilled and as powerful as we are, we can construct a reality that enables us to remain 'true to ourselves' and true to the children we are responsible for.

The radical feminist Andrea Dworkin (1982) makes the critical distinction between 'truth' and 'reality.' From her feminist perspective she perceives the 'truth' of gender equality but the 'reality' of patriarchy and gender inequality. In the world we live in, the reality she describes is that men are in control of the institutions, of personal and political power and women are, at best, under-represented, and, at worst, subjugated. The reality she goes on to describe is that there should be an equal distribution between the genders and that such imbalances and inequalities have no scientific reason to exist. I believe that this powerful concept is transferable. While the demands that are sometimes placed upon us as practitioners and that distract or compromise our values and principles are 'real', they are not 'true'; they are realities but not truths. While an 'outsider' may create an atmosphere of compliance anxiety, this is neither 'true' nor helpful to the important job that we do. Practitioners need to empower themselves with knowledge, understanding, and access to research and the emerging consensus of what *matters* to children, and be prepared to defend and challenge issues around this. Although we will always need to be aware of the reality of this, we can, and should, be able to convert this to the truth.

 Reflective task

> Examine your own approach to making decisions as a practitioner. What influences these, and are these influences 'internal' or 'external'? Do the decisions you take ever compromise your own beliefs and values as an Early Years practitioner?

Further reading

Gooch, K. (2010) *Towards Excellence in Early Years Education: Exploring Narratives of Experience*. Abingdon: Routledge.

Lindon, J. (2012) *Reflective Practice and Early Years Professionalism: Linking Theory and Practice (LTP)*. London: Hodder.

Rose, J. and Rogers, S. (2012) *The Role of the Adult in Early Years Settings*. Maidenhead: McGraw Hill.

6

Establishing Eight Principles for Effective Early Years Assessment

> This chapter will:
> - Examine the principles that underpin effective assessment
> - Establish eight key aspects that contextualise effective Early Years assessment

In the previous chapters of this book we have explored definitions of assessment – the knowing and understanding of children – and identified aspects of some of the misplaced mythology that surrounds it. We have clarified its purpose as gleaning information with which to support, challenge and extend children's learning and development and discussed the important role that it plays is defining and supporting curriculum and pedagogy. We have also identified what are the likely area of learning and development that could be termed 'significant' or appropriate 'signifiers' of children's learning, and the critical role that the practitioner plays as a value-driven expert and professional in supporting and facilitating children's progress. These aspects will underpin any approach to assessment and form the considerations and conclusions that practitioners draw on when shaping and refining their own methodologies.

In subsequent chapters I will further explore how these aspects are translated into everyday practice and the how the different features of assessment are shaped by them. Finally, we will explore the nature, content and mechanisms of assessment in the revised Early Years Foundation Stage and how this supports and is supported by interpretations of principled and effective assessment.

However, in this chapter I intend to identify eight separate principles that will need to underpin these aspects. They are drawn from a consideration of the theoretical and philosophical aspects that have been explored in the previous chapters.

1. Assessment needs to be accurate and authentic

Taking the definition of assessment as 'the knowing and understanding of children' and acknowledging that its purpose is primarily to support children's learning and development, inaccurate assessment has neither worth nor purpose. Practitioners deal with the reality of children as they are, and acknowledge their development wherever it is upon any spectrum and within any set of beliefs. If the information perceived and any judgements made or conclusions drawn as a result are not wholly based on this then the whole process becomes futile. External pressures – especially from 'outsiders' – may sometimes influence such judgements, either to 'up' the assessment to meet a target, or depress it to ensure a more favourable trajectory of progress. Either way, the primary and most adversely affected casualty of this will be the child themselves, and as a result he or she will be subject to unreasonable and inaccurate high or low expectations. The importance of challenge, appropriate support, the pedagogical process of creating 'manageable difficulty', and Vygotsky's Zone of Proximal Development, will be adversely affected. Care must be taken too that adult-driven assumptions about children's thinking, conclusions or intentions do not override and unduly influence the accuracy of what is really happening.

Part of this authenticity will rely on assessments being drawn predominantly from practitioners' observations of children engaged in their own, child-initiated, activity. In these contexts, where children experience high levels of motivation and 'ownership', they are much more likely to demonstrate 'real' knowledge, skills and understandings, in that they will utilise and apply them in a sincere, internalised way. The 'ticklist' culture derived from entirely adult-directed formalised 'testing' activities that has historically crept into Early Years practice is an unreliable way of gleaning information about what children 'really' know and what they 'appear to know' when confronted by an adult's request. If knowledges, skills and understandings are not clearly and coherently applied to everyday play, if they are not a feature of the child's self-initiated, self-motivated activity, then doubt must be immediately cast onto whether the learning is securely 'embedded', real or significant.

Equally, assessment must ensure that it takes into account all aspects of children's learning and development – both in terms of content, the defined 'bodies' of knowledge, skills and understanding, and learning 'behaviours' with which children utilise and apply the content. Sometimes referred to as a 'holistic' view of children's learning, this ensures that separate aspects of children's learning and development are not viewed and perceived with inappropriate disproportionality and unduly affect the 'knowing and understanding' of the child. Again, external pressures are often brought to bear on this, and practitioners' own 'compliance anxiety' (see Chapter 5) sometimes compromises what should constitute a truly authentic 'rounded' – and therefore accurate and authentic – picture of the child.

Any authentic view of a child will necessarily require multiple perspectives in order to be accurate, and to truly reflect all that is known about the child in a range of different contexts and scenarios. Different relationships and different adults in different roles will invariably impact on how children demonstrate knowledges and skills, their levels of confidence and self-assertion, and their well-being and levels of involvement and engagement. All of these aspects will affect and colour perceptions of the child and provide different kinds of information that will feed into and be fed by the bigger, broader picture. All adults who work with the child will need to be provided with opportunities to contribute to this overall picture. In particular, views of parents will be critically influential in supplying more embedded comprehensive information about the child's activity in a home context, where aspects of learning are likely to be demonstrated. Equally, the perception of the child themselves, with their own understanding of their learning needs, strengths, interests and aspirations, needs to be considered as a fundamental dimension of authentic assessments.

2. Assessment needs to reflect knowledge and understanding of child development and the way children learn

The decisions taken by practitioners during the assessment process need to be informed and rooted in the evidence of what is significant and important in children's learning. Rather than focusing on what is merely easy to see, or what constitutes a convenient or expedient 'logging' of information, practitioners need to familiarise themselves with the wealth of information from studies and research that shape the aspects of learning and development that resonate most strongly with sustained and sustainable on-going development, achievement and success. Equally, they will need to draw upon their own expertise and knowledge of the children they work with, their families, experiences and the communities of which they are a part. Identifying and being aware of these pertinent 'signifiers' and developing a sense of what is truly important, in the broadest sense, will enable practitioners to ensure that assessments are focused on these aspects and that processes, methodologies and practitioners' intuitions become shaped and moulded to support effective outcomes and aspirations. What practitioners choose to see and hear will ultimately be strongly influenced by this and their 'value prism' will be, in part at least, shaped by these kinds of knowledges.

Within the on-going process of assessment, practitioners also need to continually acknowledge that children are individual, idiosyncratic, unpredictable and often non-sequential or apparently illogical learners. Many of the aspects discussed in Chapter 4 directly point to this as a continual feature of working with young children; it has equally been discussed that children's learning and thinking is not always readily apparent, and part of the role of assessment is to 'get under the skin' of where the child's cognitive processes are heading. Therefore, in practitioners' approaches to assessment, a flexibility of thought and perception will be imperative. The process of 'tuning in' to children's individuality and recognising the different ways that children express their learning will be vital to ensure that the principles of accuracy and authenticity are achieved.

3. Assessment needs to fully reflect the values of the practitioner

As practitioners engage in all aspects of the assessment process, they are viewing what is seen or done through a distinct and individual 'value prism'. This is the result of their own beliefs, philosophies and experiences and informs and shapes their own approaches to all aspects of pedagogy, of which assessment is one. Practitioners need to be constantly aware that this influences their decision making, what is seen and the conclusions and judgement that result from them. This is an inevitable dimension of the practitioner's role and needs to be viewed and considered as such. Reflective behaviour, attendance on courses, continuing professional development, access to new research and their own experiences will modify and refine these values and give practitioners a more informed and 'rooted' context. However, practitioners, whilst being aware of their values as personal, individual and subjective, must embrace the necessity for their presence in determining their approaches to assessment. This is important because it will impact directly on practitioner behaviour and decisions in regard to how and what is assessed.

4. Assessment needs to be driven by the professional

Decisions about what is assessed and how this information is gleaned need to be dependent on the practitioner who is taking them and should not be subject to compromise and dilution from external pressures. Assessments, as part on of-going pedagogy, need to be informed by and inform real, dynamic, day-to-day scenarios and situations that enable practitioners to effectively support children's learning and development. The authenticity and accuracy of assessments will inevitably be driven by the practitioner's own knowledge, both of the child and the necessary skills, knowledges and understandings that they will require to be successful.

5. Assessment must have a clear purpose to support provision and pedagogy

The value and potency of accurate, value-driven assessment is to appropriately inform and support future possibilities in children's learning and development. It is not a stand-alone, detached exercise, but woven into and driven by on-going pedagogy and practice. Assessments need to specifically and implicitly extend the practitioner's knowing and understanding of children and inform their interactions through the gleaning of relevant and significant information. Assessments need to relate directly to planning and the understanding of both children as individuals and the future developments for learning. Where this is not the case practitioners need to seriously challenge and address both the content and nature of the assessments that they are engaged in.

6. Assessment must be manageable

Processes and approaches adopted by practitioners need to be manageable and appropriate, with the aim of informing the 'knowing and understanding of the child'. What is physically recorded or documented by the practitioner is a matter of professional judgement and there needs to be an acute awareness and understanding of the fact that the quality, accuracy and usefulness of assessments are not related to the amount of physical evidence that the practitioner has stored. The purpose of recording and documenting is to enable the practitioner to access the knowledge that they have on individual children's learning and development, and their acquisition of specific and pertinent knowledge, skills and understandings.

7. Assessment must incorporate a means for accountability

Stemming from the practitioner's formative use of their assessments, and based on appropriate significances and signifiers, the results, conclusions and analyses of these are usable in order to provide accountability for the impact of approaches to pedagogy and provision. The internal accountability that reflective practitioners will continually process as they evaluate children's development, the impact of provision, strategies and approaches will form the most coherent basis on which further decisions, actions and developments take place. In addition to this, practitioners will need to be aware that external accountability, in a range of forms, will be required at different points and from different perspectives and agendas. This type of accountability, although appropriate and valid, needs to be driven and articulated by the existing assessment that practitioners use, and should not create specific ways or models to do this that are not usable within their own accountability practises and that do not support their on-going practice.

8. Assessment must take account of ethical considerations

Part of practitioners' responsibility, and indeed their values, is to ensure that approaches to and the products of assessment exist within a clear ethical framework. This could be argued as synonymous with a respectful approach that takes into account what could be described as 'moral considerations'. In its application to assessment this would have implications for a number of areas and activity. For example, practitioners will need to consider carefully how children are described in any records, notes and documentation that they choose to keep and ensure that these are accurate and sensitive to the nature and needs of the child. Additionally, practitioners and settings will need to embrace the importance of sharing assessment information with parents and carers in an honest, collaborative and transparent manner. The nature of observational assessment itself and the presumptions that can surface in any subjective activity also need to be carefully reflected on by practitioners, and a conscious awareness that an authentic view, regardless of circumstantial contextual aspects, needs to be established. Finally, ethical considerations need to take into account what the purpose of assessment is and who the assessment benefits. It could be argued, for example, that when assessment is driven by 'external', 'outsider' demands for expedient rather than accurate data, that does not clearly support the real needs of the child's learning and development, then it has become an intrinsically unethical activity.

Reflective task

How well do these principles underpin and reflect your own approach to assessment as a practitioner?

Further reading

DfES (2007) *Creating the Picture*. London: DfES.

7

Assessment in Practice

This chapter will:

- Explore the conditions necessary for effective assessment in Early Years settings
- Explore the role and importance of observational assessment
- Discuss the importance of multiple perspectives contributing to accurate and authentic assessment
- Discuss the practical nature of formative and summative assessment
- Explore tensions and issues relating to the principles of effective and manageable record keeping and documentation
- Discuss pertinent aspects of accountability and demonstrating progress in the Early Years

So far, we have explored in detail the theoretical, philosophical ethical aspects of the assessment process – its purpose, uses and the considerations that practitioners make when they are involved in the decisions required. We have explored the nature of what 'matters' to children in terms of their sustainable development the likely prerequisites for life-long learning, and the external pressures that often threaten to 'dilute' or compromise the reality of principled effective Early Years practice and provision. I have identified eight principles of operation that should underpin approaches to effective assessment. Throughout, I have continually reasserted the importance of assessment in defining and facilitating good outcomes for children; how its value driven process and its content – culturally and politically identified – have a life-bearing impact on the children that practitioners work with. Assessment –

'knowing and understanding children' – is a critical pedagogical behaviour that enables effective practitioners to identify and support the key 'signifiers' or significances of children's learning and development that research has indicated form the basis of successful lifelong learning.

In this chapter I will be approaching how we then translate all of these principles, philosophies, knowledges, understandings, informed intuitive behaviour and values into everyday practice.

What then, are the aspects and considerations that surround the assessment process and the decisions we take as practitioners? What are the practical implications of these and how do we, as practitioners, secure them within our broader pedagogical skill set and body of knowledge? How does the process of assessment locate itself within the realities of the everyday?

Below, I have identified and explored seven specific dimensions or aspects of the assessment process, explored the practicalities in detail and also provided some examples and case studies of how this might appear. It is important to note that these examples are not definitive templates to be copied in any way, but are examples of how the specific dimension being considered has manifested itself in a particular setting, at a particular time within the personal pedagogy of a particular practitioner; it is the nature of the information and how it is then applied to pedagogy that is the focus, not the particular manner in which it has been presented.

1. Establishing the conditions for effective assessment

The accuracy and authenticity of assessment, crucial for its effective and applicable use, depends on the 'conditions' of the setting being suitable and appropriate in order to allow this to happen. This will mean that key decisions for the operation, management and leadership of the setting and the aspects that surround it will strongly influence the types and nature of learning and development that take place. Knowing and understanding children will always depend on the opportunities available to them, and the 'climate' of the setting being appropriate in order for significant and relevant learning and development to be demonstrated. The consideration of these 'conditions' can be further subdivided as follows:

a. **An appropriate ethos** is one in which children realise that their learning – especially self-initiated – is strongly valued and supported by the practitioners. It also needs to encompass the child's knowledge of the expectations and values that lie at the core of the practitioner's pedagogy. Where a strong, positive, supportive ethos prevails, and where this is evidently implicit and made explicit to the children, opportunities to explore, take risks, use different resources, ask questions, make hypotheses, make mistakes and co-operate with adults and peers are more likely to be in evidence. Given the important role that learning 'behaviours' play in on-going and later outcomes, it is crucial that an ethos that is warm, caring and supportive, non-judgemental, flexible and informed is established. In this environment, or these 'conditions', well-being, involvement and creativity are more likely to flourish and therefore children will be able to operate at levels of development that fully demonstrate the knowledges and understandings that have been 'embedded'.

b. Part of this overriding ethos is the support for **following and facilitating children's interests and fascinations**. To operate at the highest cognitive level, the motivation, desire and the need to achieve, solve a problem, represent an idea, and communicate a concept or thought need to be seen as central. By ensuring that a particular idea or interest is not only valued, but supported, extended and enriched with additionally appropriate resources and stimulation, children are more likely to 'push themselves' out of their comfort zone and into the 'unknown' where they will need to draw deeply from existing knowledges and understandings. When this level of challenge is apparent in children's learning, when they demonstrate what Laevers and Declercq (2012) describe as 'high levels of involvement', then the 'knowing and understanding' of the child, the assessment, will demonstrate a high level of relevant and embedded significances and 'signifiers'. The case study below and the related sequence of photographs illustrate an example of how one teacher identified a group of childrens' interest in replicating their experience of a market and how this was supported and extended to optimise opportunities to demonstrate 'significances' in their learning.

Case study

After observing the children putting various resources from outside into the cardboard boxes, it was clear that this was developing into some kind of shop. The children were sorting the objects into the boxes, asking questions about cost. I asked them what kind of shop it was and they replied 'Its Skeggy Market' (Skegness Market).

The following morning I placed a till in the outside areas resting on the 'puppet show' frame and let the children lead their own learning.

c. Fundamental to the facilitation of children's interests is **high quality adult interaction** that enables practitioners to stimulate ideas, provide provocations, ask questions and gently 'tease out' the knowledge and understanding that is present. The EPPE description of 'Sustained Shared Thinking' that enables a genuine co-constructed and mutually respectful conversation to take place around a generally child initiated theme or idea further enables children to draw on what they know and apply it fully in the situation. Although accurate and authentic assessment is dependent on the observation of predominantly child-initiated activity, the 'interchangeable flow' between this and adult-directed, and/or adult-supported activity is also a critically important part of the process of establishing accuracy. Careful distinctions will need to be made by practitioners between what is 'demonstrated' in episodes like this in order to support the knowledge and understanding of the child, and what is 'provoked', 'taught' and 'supported'. Although these will necessarily overlap in the 'interchangeable flow'; it will inevitably have implications for conclusions drawn and, where appropriate, judgements made, especially with regard to any summative assessment that results from it.

d. In order to demonstrate the skills and knowledges that are significant, the setting's **environment** needs to ensure that as it supports children's learning and development it also enables them to demonstrate what they know. For practitioners this will have implications for how the setting is organised and the availability of equipment. For example, this will lead to inevitable considerations as to how resources will need to be stored and whether or not they are accessible and linked to Areas of Provision. In order to demonstrate learning behaviours such as independence and responsibility, resources in the setting need to be accessible and usable in such a way that children can access and return to them independently. As they do this, they are again likely to retain and develop an intrinsic self-motivation that will necessarily 'pull together' knowledges and understandings. Where environments are too restrictive and adult dependent, children are less likely to engage in the kinds of high-level self-initiated activity that authentic assessment is so reliant on.

e. Equally, the kinds and nature of the **resources** will also have a bearing on whether the conditions for assessment are optimised. Practitioners will need to consider if the resources that they have chosen, especially the ones that are available as part of Continuous Provision, are open-ended, applicable and transferable to different situations and can be used in different ways. Through their on-going interaction with children and their understanding of needs, interests and fascinations, practitioners will be able to supplement Areas of Provision with additional resources or tools that again enable children to follow ideas and thus demonstrate additional, significant aspects of their learning.

The following two images represent an approach to the organisation of the indoor environment for younger and older children in Early Years settings that ensures appropriate accessibility, stimulation and flexibility of resources have been established.

Figure 7.1 Examples of continuous provision

f. In order to sustain and follow an idea, to think at the depth required, to take risks and fully explore a concept, children need **time**. The implications for practitioners and settings is to ensure that routines are appropriate and necessary and do not interfere unduly with children's opportunities to think in depth. Obviously there will be non-negotiable parameters to this, but children learn quickly that if time is always going to be limited, or broken up quickly, that there is no point in taking things further as this will only result in further frustration. Accurate assessments will necessitate the observation of children in sustained periods of activity within which moments of demonstration, responses to adult interaction and the sudden expression and realisation and application of knowledges and skills become apparent.

g. Finally, alongside time, the importance of **space** is also a consideration for practitioners. The flexibility of furniture, different areas and how resources 'feed' them will again impact on what skills might be demonstrated and what children's activity and behaviours tell practitioners about their learning. Additionally significant and impactful is the access and quality of the outdoor learning environment that will offer opportunities for children to work in different ways in different scales and with different materials that would not be possible in a singularly indoor environment. The information that this will supply will again add significantly to the authentic accurate view of the child.

 Reflective task

Consider your own environment and the prevailing ethos that exists in the setting in which you work. How does this optimise opportunities for children to demonstrate knowledges, understandings and learning behaviours?

2. Observational assessment

The notion of observational assessment has long been at the heart of effective Early Years provision and viewed as the key methodology by which accurate information about young children is gleaned. The watching and understanding of children as they engage in predominantly self-initiated activities is the means by which practitioners make their value-driven judgements about all aspects of children's learning and development. Critics of this approach have argued that it does not provide clear and objective information and therefore is not suitable. However, what lies beneath this argument is that the information is not always clear-cut or easy to 'numericalise' and therefore not easily usable in a simplistic strategic way. Children's learning is complex, unpredictable, untidy and nonlinear; if we are to accurately describe and understand this it is unlikely that we can reduce it into a simple 'score' or number. Many of the aspects that really matter, and are real 'signifiers', are not 'measurable' in this manner. The alternative to observational assessment is the traditional 'testing' or adult-driven 'ticklist' approach. In this, children are directed to respond to particular questions or challenges posed by practitioners. However, we know that this is far less likely to produce accurate and authentic information as Early Years children are less likely to be motivated in this scenario and less likely to be working at the highest cognitive level. The kind of information this produces merely represents a moment in time when a child is responding to what they might feel is the sometimes bizarre request of the practitioner. In many cases the child will seek to 'appease' the practitioner as quickly as possible and then return to the much more interesting and motivated world of their own self-initiated play; the example cited in Chapter 1 of the child in the Travel Agents is an explicit example of this. Reliance on these kinds of methods is not only an ineffective use of time and an unhelpful message to children about the relative values of adult-directed and child-initiated activity, but also these methods do not produce information that fully supports the complexity and individuality of children's learning development.

When children are observed in their play, when the conditions cited above are fully embedded, children draw from their experiences, their taught knowledges and skills, their perceptions and interpretations of the world, and utilise their learning behaviours to achieve their goals and follow their interests and fascinations; such play encapsulates all five categories of learning described by Säljö (1979). This highly motivated activity is where the highest level of thinking takes place, where children apply everything to converge on the moment in time. This then, however difficult to analyse, is the point at which significances and 'signifiers' are most present – even if they are not obviously and measurably apparent.

Observational assessment is a skilled and skilful process of entering the child's world to understand how this thinking is developing, what is perceived, known and intended; it is not clear-cut, straightforward and tidy but complex and it requires high levels of interpretation.

In the first chapter I referred to some of the 'mythologies' around assessment that have established themselves in the psyche of practitioners over recent times. One of the most enduring of these are the beliefs around definitions of observational assessment and how this needs to be managed and organised. In some cases, practitioners have devised 'timetables' of observations, where individual children are observed intensely for specific periods of time on specific days and the resulting narratives used as their assessment data. Practitioners will carefully set themselves in a corner, clipboard in hand and write down everything that the child does. Often these prolonged sessions not only deprive the children of important interaction but provide little useful or new information; if the 'window' of time doesn't coincide with a significant moment in the child's learning and development – and these moments are often sudden and unpredictable – then the information gleaned will merely confirm what the practitioner already knows and understands.

There is a place for these prolonged 'detached' types of observation, which I will explore below, but practitioners must take decisions around assessment based not on what they think is expected of them as the result of external pressure, but what will most inform them about the children – what most enables them to 'know and understand' children as learners. This will vary from child to child and from situation to situation; some children will provide information as a continual narrative and others might be more 'secretive' about their activity. The issue, or the importance here, is not the amount of time spent in 'detached' observational mode, but how well the child's learning is understood. The decision for this rests with the practitioner and their knowledge of the children in their settings; this cannot and should not be externally driven or defined.

It might be helpful then, at this point, to define the nature of observational assessment and the considerations practitioners need to take in order to manage them effectively and meaningfully.

Although the term 'observational assessment' is a broad all-encompassing term, it is important to distinguish the two specific subtypes within it.

The first of these might be termed as **'instantaneous observations'**. These are the 'micro moments' in children's activity, when they do, say or show something that, as the practitioner who knows them recognises, is significant for that child. Added to this, the practitioner will refer to their own concepts and knowledge of what is 'significant' in the child's activity that resonates with either 'bodies of content', learning behaviours, or both simultaneously. There is no formula or ratio for this, and at different stages and periods in children's development there may be many or few of these in each session. Typically, they are very short in time and the 'significance' is often hidden within a plethora of other actions and behaviours; it is the practitioner's knowledge of the child, and *their* identification of what is significant that defines the observation. Part of the skill in this context is the practitioner's ability to precisely identify such instances and moments. Sometimes these will happen during the 'interchangeable flow' of interaction between the practitioner and the child. Sometimes these will be as the result of something 'noticed' on the periphery of vision that resonates with the practitioner's understanding and knowledge of the child. These instantaneous observations are the main way in which information – data – about children is gleaned, and the overall picture – the knowledge of the child – is made from the multitude of these observations that happen throughout the year. In the example illustrated by Figure 7.2, short moments of significant activity are recorded by the practitioner as they occur. In the example shown in Figure 7.3 a practitioner notices the significant language used by a child in describing a particular aspect of their construction.

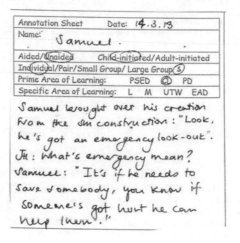

Figure 7.2

Additionally, there are what might be termed '**extended** or **detached observations**', which have been referred to above. These are the more prolonged opportunities that practitioners take to explore children's learning in more critical depth. In order to fully understand the nature and trajectories of children's individual understanding and application of knowledges, there are times when the practitioner does need to adopt an approach that 'detaches' themselves from the activity in order to fully absorb and analyse what is happening. Often, an in-depth narrative of what the child does will occur and this will again be used to inform the practitioner's knowledge of the child as a learner. In the following examples Figure 7.4 provides a detailed view of a child's exploration of a treasure basket, noting the 'significances' in their learning that are evident and identifying the next steps for development. In Figure 7.5 a practitioner records the details of a conversation with a group of Reception-aged children about the qualities of ice cubes that had been left in the freezer overnight and were now being explored by the group. This enabled the practitioner to identify key aspects of the children's understanding and their use of language. To further contextualise the experience, it had helpfully been snowing during the morning of the discussion.

Name of Child: Kiara   Age: 14 months   Obs No: 1

Date: 22.04.13   Observer: Leah

Kiara is playing in the home corner. She is holding a wooden spoon in her right hand and is using the spoon to stir the contents of the metal pan in front of her. Kiara looks at me and giggles when the spoon bangs on the metal. Kiara walks towards me with the spoon still in her right hand and lifts the spoon up to my mouth. 'Yummy' I say. Kiara smiles at me. 'mmmm' she says.

Area of Learning and Development:

Personal, Social and Emotional	Physical Development	Communication and Language	Literacy	Mathematics	Understanding the World	Expressive Arts and Design

Next Steps:
Spend time with Kiara exploring different resources eg texture and taste.

Name of Child: Kiara   Age: 14 months
Obs No: 2

Date: 24.04.13   Observer: Leah.

Kiara is looking at pictures of her family. She points at the picture of her daddy 'Dada' she says. She picks up the picture and brings it very close to her face. She smiles and shows me the picture. 'Dada' she shouts. She claps her hands and laughs. She takes the picture back and kisses the picture.

Area of Learning and Development:

Personal, Social and Emotional	Physical Development	Communication and Language	Literacy	Mathematics	Understanding the World	Expressive Arts and Design

Next Steps:
Introduce picture books with Kiara to further develop communication and language.

Figure 7.3

As stated above, there has been a dominant mythology that these kinds of observations are assessment and the effectiveness of the approach to assessment can be measured as a direct correlation between the volume of these completed observations. This is not the case, as it is the quality, usability and relevance of these observations that define their usefulness. Although they will contribute to the understanding of children, it is, as stated above, a matter for the practitioner to decide when such an observation will be necessary and to balance the decision of how much time this will involve – time when interaction with children will not be possible – and the usefulness of the resulting narrative.

Observation and Assessment

Children develop at their own rates, and in their own ways.

Playing and Exploring, Active Learning and Thinking Critically support children's learning across all areas.

Name	Kiara	Observer	Loah
Area of provision	Heuristic Play		
Date: 26·04·13	Time: 1·50pm	Duration: 20 mins	

Observation (What am I doing?)

Kiara is playing with a treasure basket. She has positioned herself next to the basket so that she can reach in with her right hand and pick up the resources inside. She picks up each resource one by one and examines it closely, turning it round in her hands and shaking them, sometimes putting them in her mouth. After doing this she looks at me 'yah' she says and passes each item to me and I put them on the floor infront of her. When I put them Kiara smiles and claps 'yeh' she says. When the basket is empty Kiara pushes the basket towards me with both hands. I move the basket next to me. 'Bye bye' says Kiara and she waves. 'Bye bye Kiara' I say. Kiara walks over to me and pulls the basket back to where she was sitting. She begins to refil the basket. When the basket is full again Kiara laughs and claps. 'yeh!' she says and walks to me. She gives me a cuddle. 'well done Kiara!' I say. Kiara cheers again 'yeh!' and laughs. Kiara goes back to the basket and begins to empty it. She repeats this activity three more times.

Next Steps to Learning

continue to offer treasure baskets and heuristic play for Kiara to explore, changing and rotating contents.

Prime areas	Links to the EYFS	Specific areas
Personal, social and emotional development		Literacy
Making relationships		Reading
Self confidence and self awareness		Writing
Managing feelings and behaviour		Mathematics
Communication and language		Numbers
Listening and attention		Shape, space and measure
Understanding		Understanding the World
Speaking		People and communities
Physical development		The World
Moving and handling		Technology
Health and self care		Expressive arts and design
		Exploring and using media and materials
		Being imaginative

Characteristics of learning

Playing and exploring – 'engagement'	Active learning – 'motivation'	Creating and thinking critically – 'thinking'
-Show curiosity	-main focus for period of time	-think of ideas
-Uses senses to explore	-show high levels of energy,	-problem solving
-Engage in open ended activity	fascination	-find new ways to do things
-Show particular interests	-not easily distracted	-make links in experience
-use objects to pretend	-attention to detail	-make/test predictions
-take on a role in play	-persevere	-cause and effect
-act out experiences	-show satisfaction/pride	-make plans
-initiate activities	-enjoy challenges and achieving	-evaluate
-seek challenges		-review
-show 'can do' attitude		
-take risks, learn by trial and error		

Learning Experience	Notes following conversations with Parent/Guardians
Child initiated	Kiara is enjoying learning and developing
Adult Supported	through heuristic play. I am going
Adult Initiated	to encourage her at home.
	Parent/Guardian Signature: L. kirboun

Figure 7.4

Ultimately, observational assessment is a subjective activity in which decisions are made about what is significant, worthwhile to observe and worthy of acknowledgement by the practitioner. This exists primarily through the practitioner's personal pedagogy and 'value prism' that defines and nourishes their practice and provision. As previously discussed, this is sometimes pressured by external factors that need to be viewed in context and should not compromise or dilute the practitioner's decisions. Recognising this subjective perception of children is vital in ensuring that the accuracy of assessment is assured and that what is seen or heard reflects the reality of the child's learning. It is all too easy to make adult assumptions about the nature of the child's learning, so care must be taken to 'get under the skin' of what is happening and sometimes 'ask the question'. A child's learning and development is marvellously unfettered by knowledge, and part of the process is building up a sense of how the world around them is made and behaves. As adults we do have this knowledge from years of experience, but for children this is precisely what their on-going experiences are building upon and developing.

Lukas: Feels cold

Arriana: Smooth

Olivia: Smooth

Harvey: Cold ... smooth

Olivia: When we were standing outside on it today it was crunchy

Practitioner: What's happening to yours?

Olivia: Mine's really melting ... I've got nothing left

Practitioner: Why is that?

Olivia: because I put it near the radiator and it is melting

Arriana: I didn't even put it near the radiator and it melted ... because it gets warm here and it that's how it makes clean water. When you put it in your fridge it makes it ice ... squeezes all of the water out

Harvey: Mine's got little ... because it's been on the radiator

Lukas: I put mine near the radiator and mine's melted

Practitioner: What would happen if we put it outside?

Olivia: It would turn back to ice and if we brought it back it would be melted again

Lukas: Twice!

Figure 7.5

 Reflective task

Focus on an individual child in your setting. Eschew references or considerations of any external assessment criteria and develop a 'narrative' of what they are doing and what it tells you about their learning. Which 'signifiers' form the main focus? Are you targeting predominantly 'content' or 'process'?

3. Multiple perspectives

In order for assessments to be valid and usable, they have to take into account all perspectives of the child's learning and development to create a truly coherent and three-dimensional picture. Any assessments that inform judgements or support learning that are based on a single perspective will inevitably have a limited – and limiting – view of the child. Children will behave differently in different contexts with different adults and in different situations. Each one of these variables and possibilities can reveal different aspects and dimensions of the child's learning and development. A child's response to adults involved in their setting and provision – a teacher, a midday supervisor, a Teaching Assistant or a childminder – can vary considerably, and each opportunity presents information – data – that informs the overall picture and understanding. The different contexts also provide hitherto unavailable opportunities to demonstrate knowledge, understanding and application of significant skills and concepts. Added to this, the different value prisms involved, the different pedagogies and the different 'outcomes' expected, equally contribute important and significant dimensions.

'We work very closely with our families, and as part of this, we hold a community coffee morning when parents, grandparents and other family members are invited into school. This is an informal event, where we can chat to them and learn about the families in our school community. After coffee, families are welcome to go into their child's classroom and play alongside them; they look at their learning journeys. Any comments they wish to make can be recorded and added to the learning journeys. This has proved to be a powerful link with homes and families.

In the reception class we have a flexible start to the day. Children can come into the classroom between 8–50 and 9–10 am, and parents can stay and play or share learning journeys with their child. The staff are able to meet and greet the families and also have the opportunity to informally talk to parents about their child. Children come straight in to play, after self-registering, and one member of staff supports children in continuous provision whilst the other is able to talk to parents. We are also developing a system where parents are able to add observations to their child's learning journey'.

Figure 7.6

a. *Other adults in the setting.* All other adults who work with, observe (in both definitions) and are in contact with children will have a perspective that needs to be taken into account. Evidently, the lead practitioner, or key group worker, will need to take ultimate responsibility for collating all the different perspectives together, but it is a crucial part of the process that these other views are sought and considered when judgements or decisions are being made.

b. *Other agencies that may be involved with the child.* In cases where children are already involved with external agencies, social workers, speech and language therapists, or portage workers for example, processes need to be in place to ensure that the specific and appropriate information is professionally sought and shared.

c. *Parents/carers.* Children will spend the majority of their time in the home environment with their family members and parents/carers. This home environment is a dynamic theatre of expression where children make sense of and utilise all forms of learning. The parental perspective on this, not only important to ensure the three-dimensional view and the full accuracy of achievement, is additionally vital in ensuring that parental engagement is fully and respectfully acknowledged, as parents are the 'first and most enduring educators a child will have'. One setting described how they engage parents in their children's learning and assessment by providing appropriate contexts to supporting the communication:

Another setting invites parents to contribute to a 'learning journey' booklet that is shared between home and setting. This includes some prompts to scaffold this for parents to consider what will inform provision and knowledge of the child:

- Has your child settled into the setting?
- Does your child talk about the things that he or she has been doing?
- Have you noticed your child doing anything different or new?
- Are there things that your child particularly enjoys in the setting?

d. *Children contributing to their own assessment.* The role of children themselves in making sense of their own learning, defining their own strengths, propensities, interests and possible 'next steps', has been traditionally undervalued. Where children actively participate in their assessments, commenting on what they can do well, what they need support on, what they can do by themselves and what they need to know or learn next is a vital part of the process. Not only does this add a crucial dimension to aid accuracy, it supports the critical process of enabling children to 'metacognise' their own learning and 'track back' on how they know a fact, idea or concept. The process of metacognition has been identified by EPPE as a critical learning behaviour that sustains lifelong learning and effective outcomes. A practitioner summed up their setting's approach to this as follows:

'We are always asking the children how they did things, what they wanted to do and if there were things that they had to think about more than others. To start with they often say little but as time goes on this becomes more expansive and they talk in more and more detail about what they have done. Then, we ask them questions like "what did you find out? Could you do that before?" and then most importantly "what will you do next time? What will you need to do better? What kinds of things will you try differently?"'

Figure 7.7

Reflective task

How do your assessments reflect different views, knowledge and understanding of the child? Do you actively seek out these different perspectives and is the voice of the parent and the child themselves evident in the assessments that you make?

4. Formative assessment

The primary purpose of assessment is to facilitate and support the child's learning, to identify strengths, propensities, learning behaviours and knowledge so that the appropriate support and challenges can be individualised by practitioners. Although this is sometimes referred to as 'Assessment for learning' (AfL) the term is not a helpful one as it implies there are other equal uses of which supporting learning is merely one. Although, as discussed, there are other important ways that data from assessment can be used, it must always be acknowledged that these are 'by-products' that cannot exist in any meaningful way on their own. Therefore formative assessment – the heart and purpose of the entire process – is the act of interpreting and understanding moments and/or sequences of a child's learning and development to identify the 'next steps' and possibilities for building on and supporting this. Mary-Jane Drummond's conclusion that this is answering the question 'How do we put our understanding to good use?' is the central starting point for this (Drummond 1993). As practitioners, the gleaning through observation and subsequent processing of this information feeds in directly to decisions about what is appropriate, significant and relevant. This on-going pedagogical behaviour, built on the knowledge and understanding of the child developed through interaction and conversation, reliant on informed intuition and an understanding of what is significant, unites and draws together all aspects of pedagogy. This could be described as 'responsive' formative assessment.

In addition to the individual developmental trajectory of each child, practitioners will also use this information to consider how the surrounding pedagogy is being supported, and, as an interchange of product and purpose, how the effective conditions for assessment themselves are being both represented and supported. Alongside the information that their knowledge and understanding of children gives them, reflective practitioners will also be considering the impact of pedagogy and provision on the effectiveness of the learning and development that takes place. This could be described as 'strategic' formative assessment. For example, practitioners may ask:

- Is the ethos within the setting enabling children to fully demonstrate learning? If not then how can this be addressed? Is there a necessity to create specific opportunities for reinforcing expectations, encouraging independence and responsibly?

- Are interests followed and supported? Is there sufficient flexibility to guide and shape learning outcomes to exist within the potent fascinations that children follow?

- Is interaction supporting and enabling learning? Are responses to children such that they are 'opening up' other possibilities and 'signifiers' and does development flow naturally from this?

- Do the environment and the resources encourage high cognitive challenge opportunities to experiment, explore and risk take and so draw together all kinds of learning and knowledge that converge on a moment of thought and activity?

- Does the information – the data – from on-going assessment indicate that there is sufficient time and space for children to work in a sustained, 'deep-level' way and therefore truly challenge, extend and apply their own knowledges and skills?

The following case study describes the process of how several aspects of effective assessment practice combine to provide carefully considered and targeted opportunities to support and extend a child's learning. The 'knowing and understanding' of the child as an individual learner was the starting point for this, enabling the other aspects to converge so effectively on his development.

Case study – Following children's interests

Super Heroes to the rescue

One way I have found useful in following the interests of children in my care, is to develop their learning and knowledge through the use of PLOD – Possible Lines of Development.

In observing a set of boys in my nursery class it became obvious that all three of them were interested in Super Heroes. These boys all had their birthdays in the summer and had English as an Additional Language. They were also my lowest achievers and where finding it difficult to engage with nursery activities. They were often noisy and disruptive.

Objective – my aim was to get these children engaged in classroom activities, while also developing their personal, social, emotional and language skills.

What I did – firstly I observed all three of them and levelled their learning against Development Matters, using the Prime Areas of Communication and Language and Personal Social and Emotional Development.

All three children were just working in the 16–26 months band.

What I did next – over the next weeks I introduced enhancements in some areas of the classroom. These where all connected to the theme of Super Heroes. These included a Super Hero tray, Super Hero masks and materials for capes, Super Hero pens, pencils and crayons in the mark making along with images of Super Heroes. I also placed Super Hero annuals and comics in the book area and next to the Super Hero tray.

Next steps – the enhanced resources were gradually introduced and adults in the room were encouraged to interact with these boys, introducing vocabulary, modelling how to play and generally being a play partner. Observations and photographs of the children were made and added to our PLOD display on the wall.

What we found

One of the boys was really motivated around the character of Spiderman – he began to talk in English saying 'Spiderman me Spiderman' and went around the room weaving his webs on the other children (this was the first time we had seen him attempt to interact with other children).

Another boy showed an interest in Superman and came to nursery shouting 'Look look' as he pointed to some Superman socks his mum had bought him. This again was a child who didn't normally speak and often cried at the beginning of the nursery session.

The third child became interested in mark making. His name was Surhaan and he started to write 'S 'on pieces of paper; he became very

Continues

Continued

animated and would write the 's' and then show you a picture of Spider man and say 'me me'.

After five weeks I levelled the boys on Development Matters again.

Outcomes

All three of them had made considerable progress in their communication, language and personal and social skills. One of them had moved into the 30–50 months band.

- Super Heroes had become a class project with many other children joining in with the activities.
- All three boys now accessed more areas of provision.
- All three boys could now stay on task for much longer than before.
- The boys' language and interaction skills had improved considerably.
- Parents joined in and brought objects from home. They became involved with their child's learning.
- Boys' engagement with mark making had increased. Lots of the children where now making marks in all areas of the nursery, inside and outside.
- Other children began to make up quite complex stories involving a Super Hero. Children's role play and narrative skills were developing.

5. Summative assessment

The knowledge and understanding of children's learning that practitioners continually process and refine as part of their everyday role can be 'summarised' at any point. The principle of summative assessment is to define a point in time during the child's learning, and in that point of time describe the nature and content of what is known about the child's learning and development. Summative assessments will include all aspects of significance that a practitioner considers to be necessary and draw together all knowledges and understandings. As will be explored below in reference to recording and documenting, much of this knowledge will not be tangibly or formally recorded, but will emanate from the practitioner's in-depth 'knowing' of the child that has built up over time. Equally, the role played by other perspectives, especially parents/carers and the child themselves, will contribute critically to the 'summing up' of what is known. Summative assessments are clearly the professional judgements of practitioners and the culmination of the multitude of different kinds of information that relate to a specific child. In summarising an on-going assessment, the professional practitioner will draw upon a vast range of 'evidence' that establishes the decisions they consequently take regarding the most effective means of supporting the child's continuing learning and development.

These summative assessments can happen at any time and effective practitioners often use this as part of the process for planning, supporting and also reviewing the impact of their practice and provision.

The purpose of summarising in this way is to ensure that there is a clear picture emerging of the child as a learner, and that any potential concerns, along with the general nature of their development, are clearly viewed and available.

In addition to the uses for reflecting and understanding, summative assessments play an important role in demonstrating progress. This is discussed further in the section below.

Perhaps the most significant use of summative assessment is to support the transition process from one setting, or age-related group, to another, particularly if different practitioners then become responsible for that child. At this point, specific information will be required in order for the new practitioner to optimise the learning opportunities for the child and to ensure that practice and provision builds on existing interests, acknowledges and recognises different propensities, and understands the nature and level of skills and knowledge the child has.

As with all dimensions of assessment, it is essential that accuracy is a critical and non-negotiable feature of this. When assessments become measurements, and aspects of 'high stakes' outcomes become related to it, there can be an understandable tendency to 'tinker' with what is known to meet an external target or to fit it more neatly and conveniently into a mathematical calculation of progress. As previously discussed, the outcome of such a temptation will be to negatively impact on the child, either by lowering expectations and therefore reducing the likelihood of appropriate challenge or by falsely inflating the attainment so that subsequent expectation will be beyond what is realistically possible.

6. Recording and documenting

One of the most contentious areas in Early Years practice and the one most subject to deeply rooted and resilient mythologies is that of documentation and record keeping. Practitioners' concerns and frustrations about the amount of 'paperwork' that they believe is expected of them often surfaces as a focal area of tension. There is frequently a belief that every aspect of a child's learning has to be tangibly recorded in some way, and the plethora of written notes and observations, photographs, video recordings and so on are believed to be the most essential requirement of effective assessment. Furthermore, this is compounded by an additional belief in the external expectation that such tangible recording is required as the 'evidence' of what is known about the child and that without this excessive and time-consuming paperwork such knowledge doesn't exist.

It is important to challenge this pervasive mythology on several levels – partly because of its inaccuracy, partly because of its irrelevance and partly because of how it can undermine the expertise, professionalism, individuality and intuition of practitioners themselves and consequently impact negatively on their pedagogy and provision.

The semanticist, philosopher and scientist Alfred Korzybski once famously wrote that 'the map is not the territory' and this described his belief that 'an abstraction is derived from something, or a reaction to it and is not the thing itself'. In the same way that someone might confuse a map with the actual terrain, he argued that there can be a tendency to confuse models, descriptions, representations or the *documentation* of reality with reality itself (Korzybski 1931).

So it is important, in terms of how Korzybski might view Early Years assessment, not to confuse 'assessment' (the terrain) with 'recording and documenting' (the map).

As has been explored, 'assessment' is the 'knowing and understanding of children', a continual pedagogical behaviour by which practitioners process information about the children they work with and from this make carefully informed decisions about how best to support the child's on-going learning and development. In terms of this subjective activity, driven by values and beliefs and existing with an externally defined cultural and political context, the practitioner is constantly and relentlessly processing, analysing and utilising the information that presents itself to them.

'Recording and documentation' is a relative 'by-product' of this process, and reflects assessments made by the practitioner but it is **not an assessment in itself**. The purpose of recording or documenting assessments is to enable the practitioner to have the clearest possible view, knowledge and understanding of the child as a learner; it supports this knowledge but does not replace it; it assists in recalling and remembering information but is not a substitute for it. A critical principle here is acknowledging fully that records and documents exist primarily – if not exclusively – for the practitioner themselves as the professional 'in situ'. Records and documentation do not exist in order to 'legitimise' the practitioners' knowledge in some way, and the *amount* of recording and documentation very rarely bears any direct or qualitative relationship to the assessments it reflects. When a practitioner makes a summative judgement – as described above – this is a professional decision that draws together all aspects of the child that the practitioner considers to be relevant at that point. In making these decisions, the practitioner will necessarily draw from all aspects of knowledge (including multiple perspectives as also described above) and draw a conclusion, or make a judgement if appropriate. Much of this will derive from the on-going relationship and constant flow of information that working with Early Years children inevitably results in.

Based upon the importance of the practitioner's professional judgement and the use for which the assessment will be applied, it could be argued that there are three principles which underpin the decision on what should be recorded. It is also important to acknowledge that any recording should never be at the expense of interaction.

1. **Practitioners should record and document what enables them to fully understand the child as a learner**. As we have explored, children's learning is often complex, untidy and unpredictable. There are occasions when an inadvertent adult assumption can misrepresent or misunderstand a child's learning intention or trajectory and a moment of powerful learning can be missed. In order to avoid this and remain within the realms of accuracy and authenticity, there will be occasions – particularly during 'extended detached observations' – when recording a narrative and exploring 'under the skin' of what is really happening becomes important and necessary. Again, there are no formulas for when and how often this should happen, and it will always be a practitioner judgement when and if, and in what context, this will be useful.

2. **Practitioners should record and document what they consider to be significant**. We have fully explored the nature of 'significances' and 'signifiers' of children's learning and how these are formed partly from practitioners' knowledge of individual children and partly from what practitioners consider to be important

about their learning and development. It remains a practitioner's decision, as a result of these aspects, as to what needs to be recorded or documented. This will inevitably be influenced by the individual child, the context and the knowledge, skill or understanding being demonstrated. There are points in children's development which are sometimes described as 'golden moments' when something appears to 'click' or 'fall into place', when a sudden realisation, awareness or mastery transforms a child's experience. Sometimes in these contexts there is a place for a self-scribbled note or a photograph to consolidate and create a reference point for the first time that this has happened.

3. **Practitioners should record and document what they are going to forget**. Knowledge and memory are not the same things, and although they are cognitively interdependent, it is quite possible to know something but be unable to remember it at a given moment. The nature of working with young children is such that as practitioners we experience a constant, relentless bombardment of information, responses, decision making opportunities and practical/pragmatic considerations. As has been discussed, the role of the practitioner is a multi-faceted, complex one. Within the miasma of thinking, intuition and decision making it is quite possible that moments get lost and 'slip through the cracks' of our short-term memory. Added to this, as unique individuals, with unique brain connections and unique experiences that feed them, it is highly likely that we will remember – and forget – different incidents, occasions and situations. The importance of multiple perspectives reasserts itself strongly here, as different individuals will remember and interpret different situations that add to the 'entirety' of the picture. But also important here is for practitioners to acknowledge that if they *do* forget these moments and arrive at the end of the session trying in vain to recall something significant, then perhaps, again, the short scribbled note or the photograph might be necessary. This is not the assessment itself but merely a means to help the practitioner recall or remember what they know.

The means by which assessments are recorded and documented will ultimately be a matter for practitioners and the settings in which they work. There are no set formulas for this and different settings use different systems and approaches with equal measures of effectiveness and ineffectiveness. Some settings record aspects of information in a 'mosaic' form that includes small-scale notes of significances, photographs, extended observations and even audio and visual footage. This is then collected in a portfolio or Learning Journal, which is often the focus of the discussion for multiple perspectives and equally shared with parents and carers. The work of Margaret Carr and 'Learning Stories' also enjoy a current popularity in Early Years settings as a means of providing a detailed narrative of children's interests, fascination and development (Carr 2001; Carr and Lee 2012). More recently there has been a development of applications for handheld electronic devices that record and classify instantaneous observations through footage or text. The issue here is the skill, understanding and expertise with which such systems are used and how they support and enable the values and approaches of the practitioner. It is worthwhile reiterating that assessment is the accurate and usable 'knowing and understanding of children', not the quantity of recorded information.

 Reflective task

Review your own understanding and approach to recording and documentation. How do you take decisions on what is recorded and what is the primary influence on this? Who looks at your records and documents and do they interpret your approach, or are records and documents being produced precisely for those who intend to look at it? How does this relate to the three principles of recording and documentation described above?

7. Accountability and demonstrating progress

In previous explorations of accountability – external and internal – I have identified the numerous pressures practitioners often face to justify and be held accountable for what they do. Although this is an important aspect of the practitioner's role, and they should be reflecting on their effectiveness, it is important that this is firmly rooted in the reality of children's development and what matters – what is significant – within it. In addition to this, the 'value prism' through which the practitioner views this, their training, knowledge and expertise will also be factors. As with the recording and documenting of assessments, practitioners will need to take decisions on what this will consist of and how they choose to represent it.

In terms of the practitioner's and the setting's 'internal accountability', the key starting point for this would be clarifying what is considered to be the most significant aspects of children's learning and development and how this might 'appear' with reference to the on-going approach to assessment and how this is recorded and documented. Practitioners might consider what aspects of learning behaviours are particularly important and in addition what 'curriculum content' – knowledge, skills and understandings – are also important and critically relevant to their continuing development. The full exploration of what is significant for children that is contained in Chapter 4 would be a possible starting point for this consideration. From this, an overview, a setting-owned 'framework', can take shape. Alongside the assessments, both formative and summative aspects, a clear trajectory of development will become apparent as children develop greater mastery, acquire new skills and begin to apply knowledges and understandings in their play and interactions with adults and each other. Again, there will be no fixed panacea for this and it is imperative that practitioners and settings devise and develop their own individualised ways of doing this as it will reflect their values and beliefs and also the nature and individuality of the specific children that they are working with.

This 'internal accountability' needs to be the starting point of any approach to demonstrating progress, impact and outcome, and the requirement for 'external accountability' must be shaped by this for it to have any meaning or authentic purpose.

However, external bodies often have their own 'measures' and models for accountability, and there is often a strong pressure for settings to describe their outcomes and developments in this prescribed way – often 'numericalised' for convenience and expediency and not always related to what practitioners consider to be significant or most important. Nationally produced curricula, 'frameworks for development' or 'inspection requirements' often form the basis of this and can vary in quality, relevance and 'usability'. Where this is a statutory, legal requirement then practitioners and settings will obviously have a duty to follow them. However, it is also a responsibility to interpret these externally imposed models, and shape them around the setting's own approach to internal accountability. Reflective, creative practitioners who are secure with their own pedagogy, confident with the purpose of what they are doing, and able to articulate the impact of their practice and provision on the learning and development of the children that they work with will be skilled to engage in the necessary conversations that surround this.

Reflective task

How is the 'internal' accountability managed on the setting that you work in? How do you justify to yourself the impact and effectiveness of your pedagogy and provision? Are you confident with this and can you articulate and defend this to those who seek an 'external' method of accountability?

Further reading

Barber, J. and Paul-Smith, S. (2012) *Early Years Observation and Planning in Practice: Your Guide to Best Practice and Use of Different Methods for Planning and Observation in the EYFS*. London: Practical Pre-School Books.

Hutchin, V. (1996) *Tracking Significant Achievement in the Early Years*. London: Hodder Education.

Kamen, T. (2013) *Observation and Assessment for the EYFS*. London: Hodder Education.

8

Assessment in the Early Years Foundation Stage

> This chapter will:
> * Explore the historical context to the requirements for assessment contained in the revised Early Years Foundation Stage (EYFS)
> * Describe the key features and aspects of the approach to assessment in the EYFS
> * Provide a critical overview of how this relates to the principles of effective assessment
> * Explore practical aspects of the approaches to assessment

Historical context

Prior to the relatively recent national focus on the importance of Early Years and the associated policy developments, the approaches to both summative and formative assessment in Early Years settings varied considerably. Although there was a rich tradition of observational-based assessment in Nursery Schools, Nursery classes and pre-school provision, this was often compromised, particularly in school settings, by external pressures. These sought to establish a 'unified' whole school approach which included Nursery and Reception classes, but was often based on approaches designed for the oldest children, then 'watered down' for the youngest. This often manifested itself in the creation of a range of 'tick lists' that would be completed by 'adult direct task' assessment. These generally focused on very narrow curricular outcomes, particularly in Literacy and Mathematics, and tended to consist of an even narrower focus on phonic knowledge and number recognition. The example in Chapter 1 of the 'apple tree' phonics assessment is typical of this approach. Although the National Curriculum only technically applied to children of statutory school age (the term after their 5th birthday), it became a strong model of influence for Nursery and Reception classes in Infant and Primary Schools. It was not unusual for a 'top-down' model of summative assessment to be diluted and adapted for Early Years classes in schools with an expectation that this would be followed to ensure that a single system operated throughout the school.

The 'Desirable Learning Outcomes'

The introduction of the 'Desirable Learning Outcomes' in 1996 established the first learning and teaching framework for children before they entered compulsory schooling in the term after they were 5. Although the document was not statutory, its implementation was a prerequisite of receiving government funding under the 'Nursery Voucher' system and therefore had a quasi-statutory status and was used widely by all Early Years providers. A further possible complication depended on the date of the child's birthday and, therefore, when they turned 5 and in which term they would fall within the requirement of the National Curriculum. Children in Reception classes would technically be required to follow the Desirable Outcomes or the National Curriculum at different times and this would be as a result of their age, regardless of their level of development. The 'Desirable Learning Outcomes' document identified six areas of learning and statements (or goals) as outcomes for children as they moved from non-statutory to statutory schooling. In addition to this, the document identified 'Common features of good practice' which included the acknowledgement that: 'Children's progress and future learning needs are assessed and recorded through frequent observation and are shared regularly with parents' (SCAA 1996: 6). However, there was no further clarification of how this might be achieved and no national requirement for any form of summative assessment to be recorded at any point during children's 'pre-school' experience. The interpretation of this rested with the practitioner and the setting – possibly with support and guidance from the Local Authority Early Years team.

In June 1997, following regional pilots, the government published *The National Framework for Baseline Assessment* (SCAA 1997). This was to be a summative assessment, focused on four specific Areas of Learning detailed in the 'Desirable Learning Outcomes'. These were to be: Personal, Social and Emotional Development; Language; Literacy; and Mathematics and the summative assessment was to be completed for each child within seven weeks of their starting school. There was no single national scheme for this and different systems of both approaches and recording were 'accredited' by the government and any of these could be used. Local Authorities would then chose a particular scheme and practitioners would be obliged to use the one selected. Again, reflecting the diversity in understanding, the external pressures and the ways in which Early Years attainment was perceived, these accredited schemes, of which there were over 90 in total, varied considerably. For example, some of the accredited schemes were a series of formalised adult-directed tasks, such as identifying pictures and numbers of objects in a printed booklet that each child completed with an adult and was then scored accordingly on the responses they gave. Others were based on observational assessments that practitioners would collate over a period of time and then make a judgement against given criteria and exemplification. Some Local Authorities provided support in making and moderating to ensure a local consistency for judgements within a particular accredited scheme that they selected, and results were collected by Local Authority teams. Due to the diversity of the schemes and the means by which the information was collected, the resulting data was not published nationally.

The Curriculum Guidance for the Foundation Stage

In 2000 the *Curriculum Guidance for the Foundation Stage* (QCA 2000) was published alongside a number of initiatives to support the development and availability of Early Years provision. Again, though not technically statutory, it was strongly linked to accessing government funding and aimed to ensure a 'national entitlement' to quality provision regardless of the type of setting the child attended. It also ensured that the declared 'Foundation Stage' applied to children aged 3–5 in receipt of government-funded sessions at 'accredited' pre-school provision that included Reception classes, if a child attended prior to the term after their 5th birthday. This seminal document transformed the perception and status of Early Years and identified the ages 3–5 as a 'distinct phase' that was covered by the requirements, and thus included all children in Reception classes in a school setting, regardless of whether they were technically of compulsory school age or not.

Whilst retaining the six 'Areas of Learning', this document extensively developed the guidance for practitioners, establishing specific statutory Early Learning Goals for each, these being the 'aspirations' of attainment for the end of the Foundation Stage. Additionally, each Early Learning Goal was supported by a series of 'Stepping Stones' that suggested the 'milestones' of development that children could make as they progressed towards the aspired outcome in each aspect of each Area of Learning. The bulk of the document consisted of fully detailed information regarding each of the six Areas of Learning, providing key aspects of 'Learning and Teaching', 'Examples of what children do' and posing the question 'What does a practitioner need to do?' in order to successfully facilitate and support this. The Stepping Stones and Early Learning Goal statements, with their associated exemplification, became the de facto criteria of summative and formative assessment in all settings with children aged 3–5. The document describes these as 'snapshots of children in various contexts [that put] the stepping stones into familiar contexts' with the aim that these will 'help practitioners in assessing' by enabling them to 'identify when knowledge, skills, and attitudes have been achieved by individual or groups of children, and to plan next steps in children's learning' (QCA 2000: 5).

Additionally, the document identified key aims and principles and how these should emerge in everyday practice. Included in this were key principles that strongly influenced the approach to assessment:

- Early Years experience should build on what children already know and can do

- To be effective, an early years curriculum should be carefully structured:

  ○ Provision for the different starting points from which children develop their learning, building on what they can already do

  ○ Relevant and appropriate content that matches the different levels of young children's needs

- Practitioners must be able to observe and respond appropriately to children, informed by a knowledge of how children learn and a clear understanding of possible next steps in their development and learning (QCA 2000: 11).

The Foundation Stage Profile

In 2003, 'The national framework for baseline assessment' was removed as a statutory requirement and replaced with the 'Foundation Stage Profile'. Although a replacement, it differed significantly in that it was a single national summative assessment and it was to be completed when the child was at the end of the Foundation Stage – typically, though not exclusively, in a Reception class in an Infant or Primary School. The assessment criteria replicated the Early Learning Goals in 13 assessment scales with additional possible judgements for attainment below, or above, the Early Learning Goal derived criteria. Extensive exemplification of how children might demonstrate the criteria comprised part of the documentation alongside detailed case studies and a CD ROM of video examples. Judgements made by practitioners were moderated by the Local Authority to ensure accuracy and consistency, with the resulting data ultimately submitted to the government and published annually from 2004 onwards.

The fact that this new summative assessment ultimately produced child-, school- and national-level data, moderated by Local Authorities, intensified the status, role and purpose of assessment in Early Years settings in general and Reception classes in particular. *The Foundation Stage Profile Handbook* was explicit in establishing principles for the process of assessment and that the judgement made against the 'Scale Point' criteria 'rests on the assumption that teachers build up their assessments throughout the year on a cumulative basis, from on-going learning and teaching' (QCA 2003). The role of observational assessment and the need to ensure that the summative assessment represented the child's 'typical attainment' and was the 'best description of the child's achievement' (sic) was emphasised.

The *Handbook* also provided detailed information for using the Foundation Stage Profile in relation to the assessment of children with Special Education Needs and English as an Additional Language. Much of the documentation was also dedicated to ensuring that judgements were made as the result of taking into account all adult perspectives of the child's learning and development in relation to the Early Learning Goal derived 'Assessment Scales', and in particular that the views and perspectives of parents/carers and the child themselves formed a significant part of the final summative judgement.

Supplementary guidance issued in 2007 (NAA 2007) further clarified and extended the principles of its implementation, ensuring that its primary purpose was 'formative' in that it supported the transition to Year 1 with accurate, reliable and pertinent information that subsequent teachers would then use to 'enable them to plan an effective, responsive and appropriate curriculum'. This additional guidance also stated that the final judgements that practitioners made were to be the result of an on-going process of collecting evidence through:

• the practitioner's knowledge of the child

- information from a range of contributors

- observation of self-initiated activities

- collection of anecdotal significant moments

- focused assessments.

It also reaffirmed the centrality of observation by stating that:

> When making a judgement for the FSP, practitioners should draw on at least 80 per cent of evidence from knowledge of the child, observations and anecdotal assessments, and no more than 20 per cent of evidence from adult-directed or focused assessments. Judgements are made through assessing behaviour that is demonstrated consistently and independently in a range of situations. It will need to demonstrate the child's confidence and ownership of the specific knowledge, skill or concept being assessed. (NAA 2007)

Birth to Three Matters

Additionally, 2003 also saw the publication of *Birth to Three Matters: A Framework to Support Children in their Earliest Years* (Surestart 2003), which provided a framework for support, guidance and progression for children in settings aged from birth to 3, prior to the Curriculum Guidance for the Foundation Stage. Although it did not have a statutory status, it was heavily recommended by Local Authority Early Years teams. The core of these materials were the 'Component cards' which explored how practitioners supported and facilitated learning and development. Central to these was the generic section entitled 'Look, listen, note'. This identified the need to be aware of aspects of the child's learning and development, suggested a focus for practitioners and alerted them of specific things to look for.

The Early Years Foundation Stage

In 2008 the 'Early Years Foundation Stage' was launched and consisted of a statutory framework and non-statutory guidance (DCSF 2008). This combined the Curriculum Guidance for the Foundation Stage, which was concerned with children aged 3–5, and Birth to Three Matters, which was concerned with children from birth to 3. A single statutory framework that covered birth to 5 was designed to merge together the two documents, to update, modify and enhance the guidance to ensure that it was as effective as possible. The Early Learning Goals remained intact from the Curriculum Guidance and the 'Stepping Stones' were replaced with non-statutory 'Development Matters' – learning and development grids which introduced overlapping 'phases of development from birth to 5 and statements of 'expectation' for children at that age.

Additional information within the learning and development grids provided guidance under the headings of:

- Look, listen, note
- Effective practice
- Planning and resourcing.

The EYFS framework established four principal themes that underpinned the Framework:

- A unique child
- Positive relationships
- Enabling environments
- Learning and development.

It also referred to how a 'secure foundation for future learning' is established; some of the keys to which were identified as:

- on-going observational assessment to inform planning for each child's continuing development
- assessment through play-based activities
- a flexible approach that responds quickly to children's learning and development needs.

Assessment was specifically noted to be 'an integral part of the learning and development process' and seen as critical to ensuring that children made progress. It also stated that practitioners would make observations of children to use in supporting and facilitating this and that these assessments should be the result of on-going daily activities based on a range of contexts and different perspectives.

As a result of the changes to the statutory framework, the Foundation Stage Profile was re-introduced as the Early Years Foundation Stage Profile. Although it remained similar in structure and process, maintaining the assessment scales derived from the Early Learning Goals and moderation by the Local Authorities, the new *Handbook* contained updated and enhanced guidance regarding the implantation and moderation of the EYFSP. This included assimilating additional guidance that had been produced and a set of video clips that illustrated 'vignettes' of children's activity from which assessment judgements could then be made.

The review of the Early Years Foundation Stage

In 2010 a review of the EYFS was announced, and Dame Clare Tickell's report, *The Early Years: Foundations for Life, Health and Learning* (Tickell 2011) contained 44 separate recommendations to 'strengthen and simplify' the existing statutory framework 'building on what works well in the current EYFS, and improving those areas that are causing problems' (Tickell: 2).

In a dedicated section of the report entitled 'Simplifying assessment' Tickell stated that 'assessment ... lies at the heart of a number of difficulties with the current EYFS' (Tickell: 2). She cites the issue of the paperwork that practitioners associate with on-going assessment and how they are 'overwhelmed by the amount .... they feel obliged to keep', whilst acknowledging that this was often a misplaced interpretation by the practitioner themselves and not a requirement of the EYFS.

In identifying and fully supporting the importance of observational assessment to ensure effective provision, Tickell also distinguishes between this and the actual recording of it, and encourages practitioners to review their own practice in this area if they are spending vast amounts of time recording rather than interacting with children. Her recommendation to address this was that '... paperwork should be kept to the absolute minimum required to promote children's successful learning and development' (Tickell: 2).

Tickell further discusses the role, structure and content of summative assessments, recommending that a new 'progress check' for children aged between 24 and 36 months be introduced to summarise their level of development in crucial aspects of Areas of Learning and particularly to identify any potential concerns and develop strategies to support them.

Additional recommendations also detailed proposals to:

• simplify the EYFSP

• review the non-statutory 'Development Matters' document

• provide more explicit support for assessing children with Special Educational Needs

• establish closer pedagogical links between EYSF and Year 1.

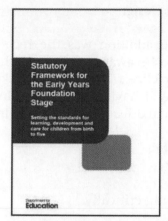

Figure 8.1   The Statutory Framework for the Early Years Foundation Stage; available as a download from www.foundationyears.org.uk

The revised Early Years Foundation Stage

Following consultations and government responses, the final revised Early Years Foundation Stage framework document was published in March 2012 and became statutory in September of the same year, replacing the previous 2008 version of the EYFS. Additional supporting materials were also published at the time – a revised Development Matters, information regarding the 2-year-old progress check and 'parent friendly' information on the new framework. The revised EYFSP *Handbook* and exemplification followed in November.

Following most of Dame Clare Tickell's recommendations, the revised EYFS retained the four principal themes and Areas of Learning.

The 'Prime areas' were seen to underpin and be fundamental to all learning:

• Personal, Social and Emotional Development

• Communication and Language

• Physical Development.

These were distinguished from the 'Specific Areas' which were believed to contextualise and strengthen the Prime Areas:

• Literacy

• Mathematics

• Understanding the World

- Expressive Arts and Design.

A radical and inspired addition was the recommendation that the framework should also be aware of the *way* that children learn and reflect this in their practice. This statutory acknowledgement of the importance of 'learning behaviours' described in the document as the 'Characteristics of Effective Teaching and Learning' were identified as:

- Playing and exploring

- Active learning

- Creating and thinking critically.

The role of the practitioner and the importance of professional decisions when interacting with children were acknowledged in the following statement:

> There is an ongoing judgement to be made by practitioners about the balance between activities led by children, and activities led or guided by adults. Practitioners must respond to each child's emerging needs and interests, guiding their development through warm, positive interaction. (DfE 2012: 6)

Unfortunately, the same paragraph then unhelpfully contradicts this with an unnecessary and unfounded statement that appears to imply, despite research conclusions (discussed in Chapter 4), that more adult direction and less child initiated activity leads to more effective learning and development: 'As children grow older, and as their development allows, it is expected that the balance will gradually shift towards more activities led by adults, to help children prepare for more formal learning, ready for Year 1'. (ibid)

In the next chapters I will focus specifically on the requirements and considerations for the statutory summative assessments: the 2-year-old progress check and the revised EYFS Profile. The remainder of this chapter will critically explore how the revised EYFS defines and details the approach to assessment as a process.

Assessment in the revised Early Years Foundation Stage

In the spirit of one of the declared aims to 'reduce and simplify' the length and content of the statutory document, the references to assessment, other than detailing the summative points, are short and concise. Assessment is clearly identified as a key pedagogical behaviour that 'plays an important part in helping parents, carers and practitioners to recognise children's progress, understand their needs, and to plan activities and support' (DfE 2012: 6) and that on-going – formative – assessment 'is an integral part of the learning and development process'. The document describes how this involves practitioners observing children in order to 'understand their level of achievement, interests and learning styles, and to then shape learning experiences for each child reflecting those observations', thus making the purpose of assessment – to know and understand children in order to support their learning – explicit (DfE 2012: 10). The stark nature of the language appeared to be driven by the Tickell findings that the perceived burden of assessment was at 'the heart of many of the EYFS's problems' and had become 'something to be done' rather than the key aspect of practice that is should be. The statutory framework then proceeds by embedding this clear sense of purpose and also making it explicit that this is the on-going process that feeds into everyday interaction and decisions, and practitioners use this assessment – the knowing and understanding of children – '… to respond to their own day-to-day observations about children's progress and observations that parents and carers share' (DfE 2012: 10). Additionally explicit within the statement, is the necessity of parental and other adult involvement, not as a token aspect but as an intrinsic part of the process itself.

The concerns regarding the 'overwhelming' nature of perceived paperwork are also dealt with directly. The perception that recording assessments had to take priority over possible moments of interaction with children is specifically identified and addressed, and the nature, purpose and validity of tangible recording is equally confronted. The statement itself could not be less ambiguous. 'Assessment should not entail prolonged breaks from interaction with children, nor require excessive paperwork. Paperwork should be limited to that which is absolutely necessary to promote children's successful learning and development' (DfE 2012: 10). While this supports the clarification of the purpose of assessment, it also ensures that the critical aspects of professional decision making – not imagined external expectations – are the key driver and most important influence in the recording of assessments. Again, within this there is a strong recognition of the interrelationship this has with parents and carers: 'Parents and/or carers should be kept up-to-date with their child's progress and development. Practitioners should address any learning and development needs in partnership with parents and/or carers, and any relevant professionals' (DfE 2012: 10).

The strong awareness of the importance of assessment to identify and support children with potential Special Educational Needs runs as a constant thread throughout the revised framework. Much of the rationale for the summative assessments, as we will explore in subsequent chapters, is driven by the acknowledgement that the earlier the intervention, the higher the likelihood of success. Additionally, there is an equally strong recognition that children whose home language is not English will need to be considered carefully and responsibly in terms of making assessments, particularly in the context of summarising this in judgement on their learning and development.

> When assessing communication, language and literacy skills, practitioners must assess children's skills in English. If a child does not have a strong grasp of English language, practitioners must explore the child's skills in the home language with parents and/or carers, to establish whether there is cause for concern about language delay. (DfE 2012: 10)

The crucial distinction that the framework urges to be made is the difference between developmental language delay and acquisition of English as a spoken language. Children who do not yet have a grasp of communicating in English do not necessarily have a developmental language delay; equally, lack of communication in English should not be a reason to dismiss the possibility of a language delay. The importance of communication with parents and an understanding of the child's ability to talk – in any, either or all languages – needs to remain clearly as the focus of this assessment.

The principles of effective assessment and the EYFS

How, then, does the approach to assessment as outlined in the revised EYFS fit within the dimensions and contexts of the principles of assessment (explored in Chapter 6) and the practical dimensions for consideration (explored in Chapter 7)? Given the deliberate 'slimming down and simplifying' of the statutory document, how does this enable practitioners to interpret the requirements to support their own 'value prism' driven approaches to pedagogy in general and assessment in particular? How does the documentation support and enable the informed and intuitive practitioner to effectively support children's learning and development?

In terms of the principles, there is much to ensure that assessments made by practitioners are **accurate** and **authentic**. The centrality of the role of observational assessment does much to establish and reinforce the concept of accuracy, what children really know, understand and can do, and the implication that this needs to derive from observation of children's own self-initiated activity should reassure practitioners that effective approaches to assessment are clearly supported. The importance of the role of parents and other contributors is stressed throughout to ensure that information is gleaned from a variety of sources. Equally, the focus on ensuring that children with Special Educational Needs are assessed within their specific context also contributes to the importance of accuracy, as does the exploration of ensuring that speaking English as an Additional Language and specific language developmental delay are not erroneously and misleadingly confused.

The EYFS framework as a whole ultimately has an ambiguous and contradictory stance towards child development and what is known about the way that children learn. It must be acknowledged that there is the welcome inclusion of the 'Characteristics of Effective Teaching and Learning' which focus on significant learning behaviours, the process and application of 'bodies of knowledge and acquired skills', and the recognition in the key principles that 'every child is a unique child, who is constantly learning and can be resilient, confident and self-assured' (DfE 2012: 3). Equally, the differentiation between 'Prime' and 'Specific' areas of learning and development and the different yet complementary roles they play in supporting, facilitating and extending children's ongoing development is a sound and clear expression of how children become successful learners. However, far less helpful is the statement that children require more adult-directed activity and less opportunity to self-initiate their learning as they 'prepare for more formal learning in Y1' (DfE 2012: 3), which compromises and dilutes the recognition of the nature of learning and child development and creates an unnecessary pressure to create an 'unbalanced' and ultimately ineffective approach. Without sufficient opportunities to use their learning in self-initiated/play activity, children's learning will not connect with their real lives nor be sufficiently owned to be secure. Added to which, polarising the language in this way, as 'either' child-initiated 'or' adult-directed is particularly unhelpful in acknowledging the sense of 'interchangeable flow' between a range of dimensions that culminates in effective, meaningful and significant interaction. Inevitably, the presence of this statement thus runs the risk that it will impact on the approaches to assessment and the means by which practitioners identify and acknowledge 'signifiers' and significances in children's learning.

Although non-statutory, the revised 'Development Matters' guidance, albeit containing useful information and support for the 'Characteristics of Effective Learning', consists mostly of overlapping age-related expectations in the Prime and Specific Areas of Learning and Development. Then, having distanced themselves from Development Matters during the Summer of 2013, reinforcing their non-statutory status, the DfE published *Early Years Outcomes* in September 2013; describing it as 'a non-statutory guide to support practitioners. It can be used by child-minders, nurseries and others, such as Ofsted, throughout the early years as a guide to making best-fit judgements about whether a child is showing typical development for their age, may be at risk of delay or is ahead for their age' (DfE 2013: 3). Although presented as a new document, it consisted of more or less identical statements from the existing Development Matters column headed 'A Unique Child' and retained the overlapping age band descriptions as what might be expected as 'typical development'. The statements that suggest what might be observed could not be considered to be any kind of definitive overview of significant child development, and many actions, behaviours and outcomes that children will demonstrate are not listed in the document. Additionally, there are a number of inconsistencies and non-sequential statements that confuse and contradict typical trajectories of development. Although, as stated, the document is non-statutory and a disclaimer on every page warns the reader that 'The development statements and their order should not be taken as necessary steps for individual children. They should not be used as checklists' there is a depressing sense of inevitability that, subject to external pressures, particularly from 'outsiders' and for reasons of expediency, they will become precisely that. Practitioners who do choose to use them as a framework need to ensure that they interpret them fully from their own knowledge and experience and creatively enhance, select and deselect the aspects that resonate or clash with their expertise.

The importance of assessment being *driven by the professional* is again both supported and undermined by the statutory documentation. It acknowledges that practitioners' day-to-day interactions will be fed by and result in observations of children and that the decisions that result from this will inform their practice and provision. Equally, it limits the need for paperwork and recording to what the practitioner themselves defines as necessary. However, returning to the statement on the weighting of 'balance between child-initiated and adult-directed activities' and the quasi-statutory status of Development Matters/Early Years Outcomes, there are serious decisions that practitioners will need to take in terms of how they interpret, modify and adapt this to protect and develop their own effective practice and pedagogy.

The recognition that assessment is 'an integral part of the learning and development process' indicates that there is a clear understanding that it has *a clear purpose to support provision and pedagogy*. The emphasis on interaction, both to generate information from observations and then to use this to support on-going development, is also a clear acknowledgment of this. The focus on identifying specific needs that underpins the rationale for both statutory points of summative assessment also clarifies a distinct and coherent purpose for the judgements that practitioners make. Additionally, the overarching principles of the 'unique child' and that 'children learn and develop in different ways' also support the necessity of effective and accurate information being used to enable children as successful and individual learners.

The integration of the assessment process as a critical dimension of on-going pedagogy and the support for the prominence of inter-action over recording support the principle that *assessment must be manageable*. There is an understanding that observations are part of everyday interaction and that the 'shaping of experiences', oppor-tunities and moments of challenge contribute strongly to the 'practicality' of how assessment is perceived. Additionally, the recognition that what is recorded, and that the how and why is in the domain of the practitioner's decision making, is another facet that supports this principle. Equally, the clear requirement that 'paperwork should be kept to a minimum' strongly asserts a welcome emphasis on a clearly manageable approach.

In terms of ensuring that the process incorporates *a means for accountability*, the statutory framework itself is more implicit than explicit in this. The first sentence in the document: 'Every child deserves the best possible start in life and the support that enables them to fulfill their potential' (DfE 2012: 2), it could be argued, is the central 'internal' principle of accountability that all practitioners and settings would subscribe to. Effective assessments will both ensure that this is carefully monitored and that modifications and adaptations to all aspects of pedagogy flow as a result of this. What is less helpful is the possibility, stated above, that the non-statutory Development Matters/Early Years Outcomes statements for Learning and Development will become a de facto measure of accountability and lead to the unhelpful and spurious 'numericalisation' of the overlapping bands to calculate progress, impact and effectiveness.

Practical considerations for effective assessment and the EYFS

The practical considerations that ultimately support these principles are contained within the short paragraphs on assessment and are also implicit within other aspects of the statutory framework.

The **conditions for assessment** are characterised in the overarching principles of the 'unique child', 'enabling environment', 'positive relationships' and 'learning and development', and much of the ethos described would be seen as supporting effective conditions for learning and observing, and that learning and assessing are interrelated and should be perceived in equal measure.

Observation, as observational assessment, is referred to throughout, and there is an implicit assumption that this is the most effective and accurate way of ensuring that assessments truly reflect children's developments, attainment, achievements, interests, fascination and learning behaviours.

The role of other adults, and especially the importance of parental contribution, fully acknowledges the need for **multiple perspectives** to feed into an accurate overview of the child. In particular, the role of other agencies in identifying and supporting children with potential Special Education Needs is a key demonstration of this consideration in action.

Within the purpose that assessment supports learning, the framework is clear on the importance of **summative assessment** as lying at the heart of effective pedagogy, and of working in tandem with, driving and being driven by, effective, appropriate and sensitive interaction.

In addition to the statutory points of summative assessment (to be explored in the final two chapters), there is a recognition that as part of the internal and external accountabilities, and in particular informing parents and carers, summarising the assessments – within the context of what, how much and when to record – is secure within the text.

Finally, as outlined in the principles, the approach to **recording and documentation** is addressed within the context of professional expertise, with a clear emphasis on practitioner judgement regarding the nature and amount of recording and documentation that is required.

Further reading

Department for Education (DfE) (2012) *The Statutory Framework for the Early Years Foundation Stage.* DfE.
Department for Education (DfE) (2013) *Early Years Outcomes.* DfE.
Early Education (2012) *Development Matters in the Early Years Foundation Stage.* Early Education.
Luff, P. (2013) 'Observations: recording and analysis in the Early Years Foundation Stage', in I. Palaiologou (ed.) *The Early Years Foundation Stage*, 2nd edn. London: SAGE.

The 2-Year-Old Progress Check

This chapter will:

• Explore the rationale and outline the requirements of the '2-year-old progress check' and consider the practical implications for practitioners and settings

The revised EYFS included a new requirement that: 'When a child is aged between two and three, practitioners must review their progress, and provide parents and/or carers with a short written summary of their child's development in the prime areas' (DfE 2012: 10).

This '2-year-old progress check' was introduced as a new initiative to provide a summative assessment of children in provision aged between 24 and 36 months. Although not described as a statutory summative assessment, the fact that it 'must identify the child's strengths, and any areas where the child's progress is less than expected' (DfE 2012: 10) does lead it to fall broadly within the definition of one.

The origins of and rationale behind this initiative lie with Dame Clare Tickell's review (Tickell 2011), and there is an emphasis on the need for, and effectiveness of, early identification of children who are 'at risk of failure' and where there are concerns regarding specific aspects of their development. As explored in Chapter 8, the revised EYFS identified three 'Prime Areas of Learning' considered vital in underpinning all development; therefore the focus of the '2-year-old progress check' was inevitably shaped around this. This in turn was strongly influenced by two documents published immediately prior to the review: *The Foundation Years: Preventing Poor Children Becoming Poor Adults* (Field 2010) and *Early Intervention: The Next Steps* (Allen 2011). These reports both concluded that where a child was 'at risk of failure' the optimum time for intervention and support was the period between 24 and 36 months. This was identified as the most effective period of time with the highest likely success rate. An additional raft of government initiatives were implemented in order to support this, with significant amounts of funding attached, and the '2-year-old offer'; which provided free care and education for targeted, vulnerable 2-year-old children was introduced in September 2012.

Consequently, the creation of the 2-year-old progress check, was designed, at least in part, to provide a means of early identification on which this approach was based.

As stated, the EYFS statutory framework required the following from all registered settings that work with children aged between 24 and 36 months:

> When a child is aged between two and three, practitioners must review their progress, and provide parents and/or carers with a short written summary of their child's development in the prime areas. (DfE 2012: 10)

It identified this age band quite specifically as the 'window' of time when this statutory assessment needs to take place. We will return later to the issues and considerations about which point is most appropriate within what will necessarily be a huge band of potential development.

The assessment also focuses quite clearly on the 'Prime Areas of Learning and Development' as outlined in the EYFS statutory framework. These areas of learning and development – Personal Social and Emotional Development, Communication and Language and Physical Development – are considered to be at the core of and as critically underpinning children's development, and as necessary prerequisites for all learning and successful development. Therefore the focus on these for the 2-year-old check, mirrors the previous pedagogical and curriculum statement that: 'Practitioners working with the youngest children are expected to focus strongly on the three prime areas, which are the basis for successful learning in the other four specific areas ...' (DfE 2012: 6).

The purpose of the 2-year-old check is made explicit, focusing particularly on the need, as defined by the Tickell review (2011) to identify concerns and possible 'obstacles' in the path of children's development that can be addressed and supported to ensure that they do not persist and unnecessarily disadvantage the child as they progress through the age bands of the EYFS and into the National Curriculum in Year 1.

> This progress check must identify the child's strengths, and any areas where the child's progress is less than expected. (DfE 2012: 6)

It then proceeds, within in the principles of effective assessment, to make the purpose of this explicit, and provides a clear responsibility for the relevant practitioner to act effectively on the information that the progress check details:

> If there are significant emerging concerns, or an identified special educational need or disability, practitioners should develop a targeted plan to support the child's future learning and development involving other professionals ... as appropriate ... It must describe the activities and strategies the provider intends to adopt to address any issues or concerns. (DfE 2012: 6)

As a key component of the assessment, practitioners are required to detail how they have responded to and supported any concerns that have emerged with the final conclusions and judgements A key component of the 2-year-old check documentation is the inclusion of approaches and strategies the practitioner has used – or expects to be used – in order to continue supporting the child's development. Where appropriate and necessary, additional advice, support and guidance might be sought from other professionals. This aspect of multi-agency working, a strong and significant thread within both the Tickell review (2011) and the revised EYFS framework (DfE 2012), will be explored in more detail later in this chapter.

It is acknowledged that practitioners would supplement the basic requirement of a description of the child's level of development within the three 'Prime Areas of Learning' with additional information that would support the child's on-going learning and development, especially if there are areas of concern:

> Beyond the prime areas, it is for practitioners to decide what the written summary should include, reflecting the development level and needs of the individual child. The summary must highlight: areas in which a child is progressing well; areas in which some additional support might be needed; and focus particularly on any areas where there is a concern that a child may have a developmental delay (which may indicate a special educational need or disability). (DfE 2012: 10)

Additional guidance was published in the form of *A Know How Guide*

(NCB 2012) which details key considerations and guidelines for identifying issues and concerns and provides pointers for practitioners to consider during the process (Figure 9.1).

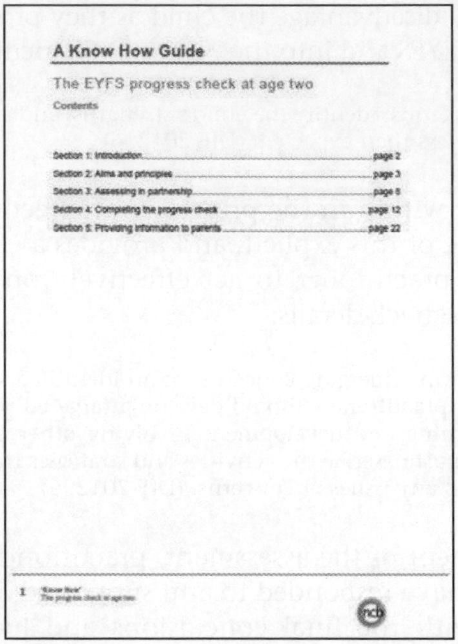

A Know How Guide

The EYFS progress check at age two

Contents

Figure 9.1   *A Know How Guide*, **available to download from www.foundationyears.org.uk**

Critically, the parent's role within this process is seen as pivotal, both in providing accurate and authentic information and acting on the outcome in whatever way this may involve. Care is taken to ensure that practitioners discuss how the summative assessment can be used in the home environment, and that, where appropriate, parents are encouraged to share this information with other relevant professionals. The actual point in time when the 2-year-old progress check should be completed is described as subject to an agreement between parents and practitioners as to the most appropriate time to do this.

Care must be taken especially when discussing the check with parents, that this is not confused with the 'Developmental Check', referred to as the 'Healthy Child programme health and development review' undertaken by Health Visitors. The latter, which focuses on health and development varies in content and approach in different Health Authorities. Originally, the intention appeared to be that the two 'checks', educational and medical, would combine into a single assessment process that would cover both, as there are significant areas of overlap, and that by keeping the child at the centre of the process the information and its use would be optimised. Although this 'linking up' of 'checks' was strongly advocated initially, it was not part of the final 'revised' EYFS framework (DfE 2012). At the time of writing there is a commitment to a future review of this:

> The Department for Education is working with health and early years experts to look at the scope to introduce a new fully integrated health and early years review at age two. Depending on feasibility, the aim is that this would be introduced in 2015. (http://www.foundationyears.org.uk)

In the interim, there is an expectation that the 2-year-old progress check will contribute to, whenever possible, the developmental check undertaken by Health Visitors, and that parents particularly would draw upon elements of both these assessments to inform the other.

The additional guidance contained within *A Know How Guide* further clarifies the aims and principles of the check, citing these to be:

- reviewing a child's development in the three prime areas of the EYFS
- ensuring that parents have a clear picture of their child's development
- enabling practitioners to understand the child's needs and plan activities to meet them in the setting
- enabling parents to understand the child's needs and, with support from practitioners, enhancing development at home
- noting areas where a child is progressing well and identifying any areas where progress is less than expected
- describing actions the provider intends to take to address any developmental concerns (including working with other professionals where appropriate).

Equally it summarises the main principles of how the check should be implemented:

- The check should be completed by a practitioner who knows the child well and works directly with them in the setting. This should normally be the child's key person.
- It arises from the on-going observational assessments carried out as part of everyday practice in the setting.

- It is based on the skills, knowledge, understanding and behaviour that the child demonstrates consistently and independently.

- It takes account of the views and contributions of parents.

- It takes into account the views of other practitioners and, where relevant, other professionals working with the child.

- It enables children to contribute actively to the process.

Care is taken to ensure that the perception of the 2-year-old progress check does not descend into a set of 'tasks' for children to perform, and it is made clear that all the information collected in order to make a judgement will emerge from on-going assessment that is essentially formative in nature. The summative aspect, the check itself, is a secondary by-product of the everyday observation/planning/assessment cycle described in detail in both the revised *Development Matters/Early Years Outcomes* and the *Know How Guide* itself.

Additionally, it again reinforces the integral role of parents, noting that an on-going dialogue should exist between parents and practitioners, sharing observations and comments, discussing likes, interests and fascinations and celebrating achievements within the principle of the importance of multiple perspectives to ensure authentic and accurate assessment judgements:

> A starting point for all assessment should be an acknowledgement that parents know their children best. They are their child's first and most enduring educators, with in-depth knowledge of their child's, physical, emotional and language development over time. (NCB 2012: 8)

The suggested process for completing the check is described in detail:

1. Practitioners, in line with the principles of effective assessment, reflect on and consider what they know about the child. Evidently, this will be informing their planning, provision and interaction, but the suggestion is that at this point a more focused reflection on the child – by their key person where appropriate – takes place to explicitly and consciously articulate and consider the child's strengths and challenges in the three Prime Areas and, as equally made clear, to identify any areas or issues of concern. How this concern manifests itself, though critical to the process, is not made too clear. It is possible that an interactive use of the revised *Development Matters/Early Years Outcomes* with the overlapping band for 22–36 months could act as a starting point. However, as explored fully in previous chapters, this would not be a comprehensive or definitive view of the multiplicity of 'typical'

behaviours at this point; so practitioners would need to draw from their own experiences, knowledge of child development and, as we will come to, the perception of others, in order to begin refining and concluding their judgements. Practitioners completing the 'check' will also need to remind themselves of the principles and practice regarding the assessment of children for whom spoken English is not their primary or home language, and be clear to differentiate between developmental language delay and proficiency and understanding of the English language itself.

2. Following this, the practitioner responsible drafts these initial judgements and conclusions, concisely summarising the key aspects and especially taking into account potential concerns, issues and aspects of development that may require additional internal – or external – sources of support. These initial comments, which will form the basis of the final 'check' need not be extensive in nature and it is expected that they would be an integral part of on-going recording – when appropriate and necessary – that the practitioner is already engaged in.

3. The next stage of the process would be to discuss these initial comments with the parents/carers, acknowledging the importance of the existing relationship and the flow of information between home and setting. Primarily, the purpose of this is to ensure that the final 'check' is accurate, takes into account multiple perspectives and particularly acknowledges the child's demonstration of knowledges and skills in the home environment. Additionally, this takes into account the clear legal position of information held by the setting about a child. The EYFS statutory framework makes it clear that: 'Providers must have the consent of parents and/or carers to share information directly with other relevant professionals' (DfE 2012: 11) as any information on the child is the property of the parents/carers and cannot be shared with anyone else without explicit consent. Therefore, this discussion serves the additional purpose of ensuring that there is a consensus on the perception of the child's level of development and any emerging concerns, and that the parents/carers have a genuine stake in and ownership of the process and the information that emanates from it. Not only does this add to the respectful mutuality of the relationship, with the well documented benefits this provides for the child, but it also heavily predicates the likelihood that parents will be willing to share – or permit the information to be shared – with other settings and appropriate professionals. However, it remains a critical point that practitioners understand that *without the explicit consent of parents/carers, the information cannot be shared at all.*

4. Assuming that there is a consensus on the level of development of the child, the key person responsible for completing the check would then discuss any issues and concerns regarding the child's development with the Setting Manager. The purpose of this discussion would be to refine and clarify any decisions and consider the implications of these. Part of this discussion would also necessarily involve establishing a strategy for support and identifying specific actions and approaches that would be appropriate. Additionally, there would need to be careful consideration of whether or not other agencies or professionals would need to be involved in order to provide specialist support. This decision would be taken by the setting as a whole and would need to be a professional consideration that relates to the nature and complexity of the issue or concern identified during the check. In this case, it is likely that this would be co-ordinated and overseen by the strategic management of the setting.

Evidently, a close relationship with the parent/carer will facilitate this process. However, it may be that there is disagreement between parents and practitioners regarding the nature of any emerging Special Educational Need or perceived developmental delay. This could arise from the parent/carer's own anxiety with the way they perceive such information will be used in the future, especially when the child transfers to a school setting, and the belief that the identification of any need would 'label' their child disadvantageously. Equally there could be a genuine disagreement over the perception of a child's learning and development, with parental/carer insistence that behaviours or demonstrations of knowledges and understandings either are or aren't evidenced in the home environment, contradicting the information gleaned from the practitioner in situ. In both cases, further discussion would be necessary. This would be to reassure the parent/carer of the use of the information and that the identification of a concern would enable appropriate support to be triggered which would benefit the child's development. A further discussion of the use and purposes of assessment information within the EYFS could also assist in allaying anxieties. Where there is a difference of perception in the child's learning and development between the setting and home environment, then this will need to be explored fully. It is quite possible that a child's behaviour may change dramatically in these different environments and it could be that the aspects outlined in the considerations for the 'conditions for effective assessment' need to be fully investigated in order to secure an 'accurate and authentic' assessment. In these instances it might be necessary to acknowledge the different behaviours demonstrated in the home and setting environment as part of the commentary within the 'check' itself.

Ultimately, the '2-year-old progress check' is a statutory summative assessment for which professional practitioners and settings are responsible. The final decisions for this, the strategies and actions involved as appropriate, and the possible inclusion of other agencies and professionals, will be made by the setting and the practitioner. The accuracy of this, particularly if concerns have been identified, must be balanced with the likelihood of parental permission for the information to be shared. However, if there is a genuine and evidenced concern, then practitioners have a responsibility to identify it; even if this is likely to result in parental/carer withdrawal of permission.

5. Following this, the progress check is completed and finalised. Although *A Know How Guide* contains a number of exemplars and completed documents, there is no expectation or requirement that a specific template or formula is to be used. Settings may develop their own approaches to this – in line with the EYFS framework's statements on the amount of paperwork and recording – or use and adapt ones that are being developed as supportive templates from Local Authority Early Years teams. The basic requirements remain that it must include comments on the child's level of development in the three Prime Areas, identification of concerns and, if concerns have been identified, which internal – and if appropriate external – actions will be taken as a result. Some of the suggested templates for recording this include the overlapping age-related bands contained in the revised *Development Matters/Early Years Outcomes*, with the suggestion that the practitioner decides which best describes the child in which aspect of the Prime Area of Learning and Development. This would immediately indicate that any child not secure with the 22–36 month band in any area would be likely to give cause for concern. Although this is an understandably sensible and pragmatic approach, it needs to be acknowledged, as stated previously, that the statements in the column of 'A unique child – observing what a child is learning' do not constitute an exhaustive, comprehensive or definitive description of a child's development and should not be used in an overzealous nor 'forensic' manner. Practitioners will need to creatively supplement, reduce and ignore the 'content' of this in order to affect an accurate decision, particularly if this involves potentially identifying a perceived need or concern.

6. Once the check is completed, a copy is given to the parents. A copy is also retained by the setting as this forms part of their on-going records and describes a point of summative assessment. Within a principled approach to assessment, whether specific concerns have been identified or not, this would continue to be used by the practitioner and the setting to provide next steps in learning and development and to enable them to reflect on the effectiveness of their provision and the impact of their pedagogy. At the point of transition to the next setting or provider, the parent/carer would have the opportunity of sharing the check with the receiving practitioner and setting. Additionally, the setting that has carried out the 2-year-old progress check may suggest that their copy is given to the receiving practitioner and setting as part of the transition process and to support effective pedagogy that builds on what is known about the child already. *If this is the case then practitioners must ensure that explicit consent from the parents/carer is obtained.* Some settings have developed formats that include an opportunity for the parent/carer to sign their consent and therefore agree to the information being transferred.

In retaining a copy of the check, the setting will also be required to implement any actions that will result from identifying an emerging concern or developmental delay. Although specifically required by the check, this would reflect on-going effective practice and pedagogy. Such actions could take the form of particular activities or approaches, or the provision of specific opportunities and experiences that will address the issues involved. It will obviously be imperative that these are then shared with the parent/carer in order to ensure that there is a seamless and self-supporting consistency between the home and setting environments. If the conclusion is formed that additional, external specialist support is required then permission from the parent/carer would be sought at this point in order to access this.

The requirement that the check takes place when the child is aged between 24 and 36 months raises issues regarding the timing. Both the statutory EYFS framework and the *A Know How Guide* are both clear that it will be a professional decision for the practitioner and the setting regarding when this is most appropriate and will optimise the purposes of the check. In order to assist in making the decision the guidance offers the following consideration:

> *The child's entry point to the setting.* Settings should consider a settling in period for a child to enable their key person and other practitioners to build up good knowledge of that child's development, abilities and interests before completing the progress check. (NCB 2012: 15)

In common with all assessments, accuracy and authenticity will need to be assured if the information is to inspire confidence in anyone who uses it. The check will not be valid if there has not been sufficient time for the practitioner/key person, to gain a confident overview of who the child is, what their levels of development are and, in particular, if there are any concerns. Children new to a setting, dealing with unfamiliar adults, are less likely to demonstrate typical and consistent behaviour until a period of 'settling in' has been experienced. Although the re-quirement to complete the check is a statutory one, practitioners will need to be confident and assured that any judgements and statements that they make are correct and justifiable. In a scenario where a child joins a setting immediately prior to their 3rd birthday, it may be that there has been insufficient opportunity to reach a decision. In this case practitioners should indicate this in the format they choose to use, and continue with on-going formative assessment, including the identifica-tion of concerns if and when they become apparent, albeit after the 24–36 month window prescribed.

> *Individual needs and circumstances.* If a child has a period of ill health or a significant event in their family (e.g. family breakdown, bereavement or the arrival of a sibling) it may be appropriate to delay the check. (NCB 2012: 15)

Again, a professional decision, in conjunction with the parent/carers, should be taken to ensure that the resulting check is accurate. External factors that impact on a child's well-being and security will need to be taken account of and the final check delayed. This will, of course, not impact on the on-going assessments and the use of them to support children on a day-to-day basis in the setting.

> *Parental preferences.* Practitioners should agree with parents when is the best time to provide the summary. Where possible, early years settings should consider carrying out the progress check in time for parents to share it with the health visitor at the two year old health and development review. (NCB 2012: 15)

In order to optimise its use, the timing of the check needs to be considered alongside its purpose. The developmental check undertaken by Health Visitors will doubtlessly be informed by the practitioner/setting response and the conclusions drawn from their on-going, formative assessments. Where this is possible, and there is parental agreement, the information could be usefully provided at this point. Additionally, if there are already emerging concerns before a child reaches 24 months, the implementation of the check, as soon after the child's 2nd birthday as possible, will immediately trigger the additional support required. Again, discussions and dialogue with parents/carers will be a key component in this process to provide a joint understanding of the best way to proceed.

Pattern of attendance. If a child has a period of non-attendance or irregular attendance then that may affect the timing of the review. Likewise, a practitioner may find it takes longer to build up a clear picture of a child who attends just a few hours per week. (NCB 2012: 15)

As with the considerations regarding the child's entry point to a setting, a pattern of infrequent or irregular attendance will provide challenges for practitioners in building up an accurate view of consistent behaviours, knowledges and skills. Again, as with any assessment, the emphasis is on accuracy and the practitioner will need to take decisions on how this unfolds. Dialogue with parents/carers will become another important dimension to consider, but, as already stated, the ultimate decision will need to be a professional one taken by the setting.

Advice is also given regarding children attending more than one setting or changing settings in the middle of the 24–36 month period. The key responsibility for children attending multiple settings would rest with where the child spends the majority of their time, though, within the context and practice of effective assessment, the perspectives of the other practitioners – possibly via dialogue with the parents – would also need to be taken into account and inform the final 'check'. Equally, when a child transfers settings the receiving practitioner would take responsibility for the check if it has not been completed. However, depending on the timing, and where the child is, age wise, between 24 and 36 months, information and support with the decision would again need to be sought from the previous setting, again possibly through dialogue and discussion with the parent/carer.

Practitioners and settings will need to carefully consider the potential uses – and misuses – of the information that the check provides. As with any summative assessment it will offer a plethora of uses, but will also be subject to some of the inappropriate misuses referred to in earlier chapters. The genesis for the idea – contained within the Tickell review – was to specifically identify and support children where concerns had been in evidence. Part of the process for this, which was more strongly articulated in the Tickell review than subsequent government responses and the final EYFS statutory framework, was for a more joined-up approach between different agencies and a co-ordinated and shared response to supporting vulnerable children. The 2-year-old progress check was to be a tangible part of this move; much of which was summarised in the document *Supporting Families in the Foundation Years* (DfE/DoH 2011).

Although, at the time of writing, there is a long-term commitment to further exploring these links, the current situation remains the same, in that the 2-year-old progress check implemented by practitioners will run alongside the 2½-year-old developmental check implemented by Health Visitors. The most effective practice will be to begin developing these links on an informal basis and to prompt generic discussions between educational and health professionals on the parameters, processes and purposes of the two different checks that are implemented at a similar time with a similar name. Ideally, and obviously with the explicit consent of parents/carers, the two assessments would have the opportunity to inform and be informed by each other, and the discussions and conclusions drawn from this multi-disciplinary perspective would benefit the overall knowledge of the child and the approaches best suited to meeting their needs.

Equally there needs to be an awareness amongst practitioners and settings that any attempts to 'numericalise' the information and begin to assert trajectories and clinical expectations related to it will be highly suspect. The 12-month size of the window in which the check can take place should sufficiently dilute any attempts to 'codify' the outcomes in some way. However, the possible use of the Development Matter bands to describe this 'attainment' could itself lead to other uses and practitioners will need to be wary of this by ensuring that the nature and purpose of the check is clear.

Examples of completed 2-year-old progress checks

Examples (see overpage) of completed 'Two Year old Progress check' for a child within a typical range of development, it includes a section entitled 'Next Steps to Support Development'.

EYFS 2 Year Progress Check

Name: K	Key Person's Name:	Parent/Carer's comment: K has achieved alot while being
Age:	TAS4	at nursery, I am very happy with her progress.
Date: June 2013		Signature: K

Your child's learning: Playing and exploring – *finding out and exploring; playing with what they know; being willing to 'have a go'.* **Active learning** – *being involved and concentrating; keeping trying; enjoying achieving what they set out to do.* **Creating and thinking critically** – *having their own ideas; making links; choosing ways to do things.*

K has done really well this term. Her interaction skills with her peers and adults and the way she engages with outside agency is excellent and shows what a confident little girl she is. She enjoys all aspects of nursery and each area exploring and learning new things. K's attendance is very good and this does reflect on her learning. She is very independent and is onead in learning.

Personal, Social and Emotional Development

Making relationships; Self-confidence and self-awareness; Managing feelings and behaviour.

K is a very friendly, happy girl. She will play alongside her friends and can elaborate ideas amongst. Xavier-Jo is a leader and her confidence reflects in this. She has a special bond with her key person and also is very outgoing towards outside agencies. She will freely communicat and talks about home and community. K now will freely share as before not as much.

Making Relationships					
0-11	8-20	16-26	22-36	(30-50)	40-60+

Self-Confidence and Self-Awareness					
0-11	8-20	16-26	22-36	(30-50)	40-60+

Managing Feelings and Behaviour					
0-11	8-20	16-26	22-36	(30-50)	40-60+

Communication and Language

Listening and attention; Understanding; Speaking.

K has excellent listening skills and especially at storytime listens with increasing attention and will recall events in correct sequence. She can follow directions even if she is engaged and focused in an activity. K is a very keen talker. Her vocab + language is excellent and very beyond her age group. Myself and K can sit for a long period of time talking about anything and her response each time is very clear and interesting.

Listening and Attention					
0-11	8-20	16-26	22-36	(30-50)	40-60+

Understanding					
0-11	8-20	16-26	22-36	(30-50)	40-60+

Speaking					
0-11	8-20	16-26	22-36	30-50	(40-60+)

Physical Development

Moving and handling; Health and self-care.

K is an active girl and moves freely and confidently in a wide range of ways, changing directions. She can travel with confidence + skill around, under, over and through balancing and climbing equipment. She shows preference for using her right hand and is able to hold pencil between thumb + 2 finger's. K is also begining to form recognisable letters. K is confident going to the toilet, dressing herself and understands the need's for a healthy diet.

Moving and Handling					
0-11	8-20	16-26	22-36	30-50	(40-60)

Health and Self-Care					
0-11	8-20	16-26	22-36	30-50	(40-60)

EYFS 2 Year Progress Check

Next Steps to Support Development:

* Introduce K▮ to her new key person for the remaining term.
* Continue to support K▮ with her everyday routine.
* More activities in regards to writing her name and initial sounds in name.
* Writing numbers 1-3
* Support K▮ with her transition to school in September.
* Continue to help support mum in encouraging K▮ to sleep in her own bed

Signed:

Parent/Carer

Signed: *[signature]* Zafar
Insa

Key Person

Signed:

Health Visitor

Further reading 📖

Clare, A. (2012) *Creating a Learning Environment for Babies and Toddlers*. London: SAGE.

Lindon, J. (2012) *What Does It Mean to Be Two?* London: Practical Pre-School Books.

NCB (2012) *A Know How Guide: The EYFS Progress Check at Age Two*. DfE.

10

The Early Years Foundation Stage Profile

This chapter will:

- Explore the principles, content and requirements of the revised Early Years Foundation Stage Profile
- Consider the practical implications of its implementation

The Foundation Stage Profile (FSP) was first introduced in 2003, as a single statutory summative assessment for the end of the then Foundation Stage, later the Early Years Foundation Stage (EYFS), ostensibly replacing the numerous 'Baseline Assessments' as a statutory summative record, though, as previously discussed, this changed the required timing of the assessment from the beginning to the end of the phase. Typically the (EY)FS Profile would be completed by the Reception teacher at the end of the summer term, as the child prepared to transfer to Y1, though the requirement that this was completed at the end of the academic year in which the child turned 5 sometimes led to it being completed by other practitioners such as childminders or Nursery and pre-school staff, where summer-born children accessed their pre-school entitlement in a provider other than a school setting and transferred directly into Year 1. Subject to some small changes and additional guidance, the FSP – rebranded though unchanged as the 'EYFS Profile' in 2008 – remained a constant within Early Years as the summative assessment prior to children beginning to access the National Curriculum.

Thirteen 'Scales' which reflected the then six 'Areas of Learning' contained nine points, partly hierarchical, against which practitioners made judgements based on their knowledge and understanding of the children in their setting. The judgements made by practitioners were then converted to a numerical database which was then analysed and published annually by the government. Driven by the principle of observational assessment, and secured by extensive and comprehensive approaches and mechanisms for moderating, evidence trialling and establishing consistency of the judgements, if often encapsulated a broader change to approaches to overall assessment in the Early Years, and many of the principles, approaches, uses of data and understanding often 'trickled down' into other areas of the (EY)FS, where the (EY)FS Profile was not a statutory requirement. It could be argued that the (EY)FS Profile became the focal point for all the concerns about approaches to and the uses of generic assessment in the (EY)FS; with criticisms of the perceived paperwork requirements, evidencing and uses or misuses of the resulting data. A wealth of guidance and clarification was issued by the statutory body delegated to implement, monitor and support it nationally – first the National Assessment Agency (NAA), then the Qualifications and Curriculum Agency (QCA), reconfigured as the Qualifications and Curriculum Development Agency (QCDA). A rigorous moderation system was developed and Local Authorities were intensely supported, with visits from 'Support and development officers' (S&DOs) and a system of accreditation for Local Authority moderators. Despite this, mythologies, misunderstandings and misuses of the information produced continued, and even though there was a widespread recognition of the (EY)FSP's purpose and its eventual accuracy, national consistency and use to support transition, an overlying perception of negativity remained.

This was acknowledged in the 2011 review of the EYFS: *The Early Years: Foundations for Life, Health and Learning* where it was stated by Dame Clare Tickell that:

> I have heard mixed and strong views on the topic of assessment at the end of the EYFS – the EYFS Profile. On balance, the majority agree we should retain a summative, or summary, assessment at the end of the reception year, but it is also clear that the existing EYFS Profile is too detailed and complex. More could be done to maximise the value of the information, particularly to Year 1 teachers. Many have spoken to me about the burdens they feel have been introduced by this assessment, through paperwork and through moderation and inspection processes. (Tickell 2011: 32)

There was strong support in the review for the need and desirability of an end-of-phase summative assessment that built on the principles of generic effective assessment in the EYFS, and a need for a national dataset that described outcomes at the point of transition to Y1. The recommendation that followed on from this suggested that: '... the assessment at the end of the EYFS, the EYFS Profile, should be significantly slimmed down and made much more manageable, based on my 17 proposed new early learning goals, and have clearer links into the National Curriculum' (Tickell 2011: 33).

The suggested replacement, the revised EYFS Profile, was to contain judgements against the newly created 17 Early Learning Goals and a 'three item' description of children's 'Characteristics of effective learning'. In an ironic display of mythology-based misunderstanding, the review stated that these '20 items' would be 'a considerable reduction from the former 117 scale points that teachers were previously required to report on', not realising, or not acknowledging, that the actual composition of the revised ELGs, while technically less in number, contained at least as many if not more in actual content. In addition to which, practitioners were never required to make 117 judgements for the (EY)FSP, as, depending on the level of development of each child, this would be refined to the level of ELGs themselves, attainment prior to the ELGs or those attaining significantly beyond the ELGs.

Acknowledging that 'Any judgements made about children's level of development clearly need to be reliable in order to guide their continued progress as learners most effectively ...', Tickell proceeds by stating that: '... I am aware there is a tension linked to the way that children's abilities are assessed for the purposes of formal reporting' (2011: 34). Referring to the 80/20 ratio of evidence gleaned from child-initiated and adult-directed activity respectively, as previously discussed, Tickell notes that there was confusion about its use and meaning, and that this often impacted unintentionally on practice and pedagogy. The report set about clarifying the language and attempting to remove the confusion by recommending that guidance simply sets out that assessment should be based primarily on the observation of daily activities that illustrate children's embedded learning (Tickell 2011: 35).

These specific recommendations were fully accepted in the final review and the resulting statutory (revised) EYFS profile was a faithful realisation of Tickell's conclusions.

The *EYFS Statutory Framework* was published in March 2012 and took effect from September of the same year. It introduced the principles, purpose and process of the revised EYFS Profile that broadly reflected in essence the one it replaced:

> The EYFS Profile must be completed for each child. The Profile provides parents and carers, practitioners and teachers with a well-rounded picture of a child's

knowledge, understanding and abilities, their progress against expected levels, and their readiness for Year 1. The Profile must reflect: ongoing observation; all relevant records held by the setting; discussions with parents and carers, and any other adults whom the teacher, parent or carer judges can offer a useful contribution. (DfE 2012: 11)

The documentation then establishes one of the most significant differences between the previous and current versions of the Profile, namely the criteria against which practitioners must relate their knowledge and understanding of children in order to make a judgement. The previous 9-point scale, consisting of single separate statements, was now replaced with the Early Learning Goals (ELGs) themselves – a much larger 'body' of content that comprised each aspect of the Learning and Development 'outcomes'. This made the framework of aspirations or expectations for the end of the EYFS exactly the same as the criteria against which they are to be judged. In this context a different type of expression or recording of the judgement would therefore be needed. The previous approach, essentially a 'criterion referenced' assessment against which practitioners would make a definitive 'yes' or 'no' judgement, taking into account the knowledge of the child and whether or not they demonstrated the nature of the criteria consistently and independently, would not be applicable. Therefore a 'best fit' type of approach, against the content of the relevant ELG as a whole, would need to be taken. This will be explored in further detail below, but the principle of this – the '3 Es' – was clearly established in the statutory framework itself:

> Each child's level of development must be assessed against the early learning goals (see Section 1). Practitioners must indicate whether children are meeting expected levels of development, or if they are exceeding expected levels, or not yet reaching expected levels ('emerging'). This is the EYFS Profile. (DfE 2012: 11)

The 'Characteristics of Effective Learning', the 'learning behaviours' that children demonstrate and the means and processes they use to apply, utilise and make meaning from their knowledges, skills and understanding, are embedded within the requirements of the EYFS Profile itself. In addition to forming part of the framework in terms of pedagogy and provision, and the necessity that planning and interaction would need to take account of and acknowledge these, alongside and underpinning the more curricular/bodies of knowledge contained with the new 7 Areas of Learning and Development, the fact that these 'Characteristics' form part of the summative assessment should not be underestimated. This imbues them with a value, status and purpose that both enhances and protects them, in addition to ensuring that the link with the knowledge and understanding of the child as learner is made explicit as they transfer to Y1.

> Year 1 teachers must be given a copy of the Profile report together with a short commentary on each child's skills and abilities in relation to the three key characteristics of effective learning ... These should inform a dialogue between Reception and Year 1 teachers about each child's stage of development and learning needs and assist with the planning of activities in Year 1. (DfE 2012: 11)

The framework also makes it clear that the EYFS profile will be a universal summative assessment for all children and that children with Special Educational Needs will also be assessed against the ELGs with an accompanying narrative of their characteristics as learners. Specific requirements will be further detailed below, though the statutory framework notes that: 'Reasonable adjustments to the assessment process for children with special educational needs and disabilities must be made as appropriate. Providers should consider whether they may need to seek specialist assistance to help with this' (DfE 2012: 11).

Equally, for the purposes of the EYFS Profile, practitioners would also be required to consider the same approaches to assessing children whose home language was not English, as throughout the EYFS in its entirely, ensuring that judgements made did not confuse developmental language delay with acquisition and fluency in the English language.

As with the previous EYFS Profile, a comprehensive moderation system to ensure accuracy and generate valid national data will support the implementation of the assessment: 'Providers must take part in all reasonable moderation activities specified by their local authority and provide the local authority with such information relating to the EYFS Profile and assessment as they may reasonably request' (DfE 2012: 11). Equally, a responsibility to submit the data to LAs on request will be retained in a similar way to previous versions of the (EY)FS Profile.

Following the launch and implementation of the revised EYFS, new guidance that specifically related to the EYFS profile was published in November 2012. This extended and clarified the description and requirements for the EYFS Profile contained in the previously published statutory framework and also provided extensive documentary exemplification for the judgements to be made for the ELGs. It is worth noting that this exemplification focuses entirely on the 'expected' level of development.

The revised handbook again strongly asserts the key principles of effective assessment as they relate to the summative assessment of the EYFS Profile, specifically the importance of assessments made through observations of children in self-initiated contexts and situations and the importance of multiple perspectives to ensure accuracy and authenticity:

Assessments will be based primarily on observation of daily activities and events. Practitioners should note in particular the learning which a child demonstrates spontaneously, independently and consistently in a range of contexts. Accurate assessment will take account of a range of perspectives including those of the child, parents and carers and other adults who have significant interactions with the child. (STA 2012: 5)

These principles are further extended and developed to provide a strong underpinning of effective assessment on which the summative outcome – the EYFS Profile – is subsequently built. It also ensures that clear definitions of the key aspects, including those which have been most subject to mythology, are included, and awareness and internalisation of this 'small print' will be vital for practitioners if the growth and development of new mythologies and misunderstandings are to be avoided.

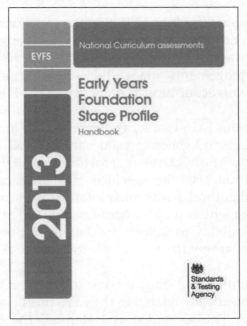

Figure 10.1   EYFS Profile Handbook available to download from www.foundationyears.org.uk

Five key principles connect all these aspects together:

1. **'Reliable and accurate assessment is based primarily on the practitioner's knowledge of the child gained predominantly from observation and interaction in a range of daily activities and events'**

The strength of observational assessment, and the assertion that this is 'the most reliable way of building up an accurate picture of children's learning and development' forms the basis on which the EYFS Profile operates. As previously discussed, the importance of children engaging in self-motivated activities, when they 'draw together' everything known and necessary for the moment of expression, communication or problem solving, is crucial to the notion of accuracy and authenticity. Equally strong within this principle is the importance of practitioner knowledge and expertise, and the acknowledgement that it is the day-to-day interaction between practitioner and child that co-constructs that knowledge and understanding on which decisions for the EYFS Profile will ultimately be based. Building on the approach to assessment in the EYFS framework, care has been taken to ensure that excessive and unnecessary paperwork and documentation are avoided, with only that which supports the practitioner in making their judgement being recorded, and that there are no specific expectations or templates in which to do this: 'Settings may choose to record children's learning in any way which suits their purposes' (STA 2012: 12). Much anxiety has previously focused on the notion of 'evidence' and 'evidencing' judgements in order to 'prove' that a practitioner's decision is accurate and reliable, and some of the excessive and unnecessary approaches to recording resulted from this. In common with previous guidance, the revised *Handbook* clearly defines evidence as: '... any material, knowledge of the child, anecdotal incident or result of observation or information from additional sources that supports the overall picture of a child's development' (STA 2012: 12), reasserting the importance of practitioner knowledge and going on to reaffirm that:

> There is no requirement that it should be formally recorded or documented; the extent to which the practitioner chooses to record information will depend on individual preference. Paperwork should be kept to the minimum that practitioners require to illustrate, support and recall their knowledge of the child's attainment. (STA 2012: 11)

2. 'Responsible pedagogy must be in place so that the provision enables each child to demonstrate their learning and development fully'

A clear articulation of the conditions for effective assessment rests again on the need for accuracy and a clear sense of what children really know and can do. 'Effective assessment can only take place when children have the opportunity to demonstrate their understanding, learning and development in a range of contexts' (STA 2012: 11). Providing for the opportunities and ensuring that conditions and approaches optimise the knowledge, skills and understanding that can be effectively demonstrated needs careful consideration by practitioners and settings. The key considerations here are identified as:

- An effective understanding of child development and how to support this

- An effective curriculum and opportunities for children to be sufficiently motivated and inspired in order to become engaged at an optimum level of development

- An environment that enables children to make choices and exercise their independence and act as agents in their own learning

- Effective episodes of high quality interaction between adults and children

- Effective organisation of resources and personnel. (STA 2012)

3. 'Embedded learning is identified by assessing what a child can do consistently and independently in a range of everyday situations'

The importance of information gleaned from child-initiated activities is again stressed to ensure that accuracy and significant, rather than 'suface level', learning is being assessed, and that it is the application and 'ownership' of a knowledge or skill and its relationship to everyday and contextualised use that define it as 'secure' rather than simply and superficially acting in response to an adult request or prompt. Anxieties related to the distinction between adult-directed and child initiated assessment and the definitions associated with them are approached and addressed, within the notion of 'embedded learning and secure development'. Although these may exist in a context of interaction, it is stressed that they are 'demonstrated without the need for adult support' and it is concluded that 'Where learning is secure it is likely that children often initiate the use of that learning. ... Attainment in this context will assure practitioners of the child's confidence and ownership of the specific knowledge, skill or concept being assessed' (STA 2012: 10).

4. 'An effective assessment presents an holistic view of a child's learning and development'

The extent to which learning and development overlap, with the judgements made by practitioners deriving necessarily from an 'interpretation' of what a child is doing, is a recognisable aspect and consideration in assessment. Although, as discussed, children do not fragment and segment their learning into neatly defined areas of the curriculum, and practitioners making judgements related to the 'significance' and 'signifiers' of their learning must be aware of this, part of the practitioner judgement will always be to identify and 'extract' specific aspects of knowledge, understanding and behaviour being demonstrated by the child. However, it is important to note that *when making assessments in general, and for the EYFS Profile in particular, the starting point must be the knowledge and understanding of the child rather than the specific criteria for the assessment*. The content of the revised EYFS Profile contains many overlapping elements, especially within the 'characteristics of effective learning' and between these and elements of the Learning and Development requirements for Personal Social and Emotional Development, in addition to the inherent links between language and all other areas. The statement in the *Handbook* that 'Seeing these links will bring coherence to the assessment process and enable practitioners to capture each child's learning more effectively and genuinely' (STA 2012: 10) encourages practitioners to start by applying the knowledge of the child to the criteria for assessment, rather than the opposing approach, which would be likely to lead to confusion and the over-duplication and interpretation of the same specific information.

5. 'Accurate assessments take account of contributions from a range of perspectives including the child, their parents and carers, and other relevant adults'

The importance of multiple perspectives is also identified as a key principle for the implementation of the EYFS Profile and the accuracy and reliability that is required. The references to the 'Contributors' also stress the importance of the 'two-way flow' of information from home to school as a key way in which the child's learning and development is understood and supported. It is stated that: 'Assessment without the contribution of parents provides an incomplete picture of a child's learning and development' (STA 2012: 10).

Inclusion

Although there is still a universal requirement that all children are assessed within the EYFS Profile, additionally there is an acknowledgement that this may provide a 'particular challenge' and specific guidance within the *Handbook* clarifies significant aspects in this regard.

For children with Special Educational Needs or a disability, there is a reaffirmation that observational assessment will remain the main methodology for identifying significances and signifiers in the child's learning and development. There will need to be adaptations and modifications for this and an understanding that children may express or demonstrate aspects of their learning and development in different ways. Additionally, specific equipment and means of communication should be treated as part of the everyday assessment process and considered in an equal way.

With children for whom English is not their home language there is a specific acknowledgement that this is not a Special Educational Need and that a clear distinction needs to be made between language development and the acquisition of English. As discussed previously, these two factors need to be treated separately and not confused either way. The clear requirement is that the Prime ELGs for Communication and Language and the Specific ELG for Literacy need to be assessed in *English* – this will be what is recorded in the summative document and will form the data submitted to the Local Authority. This does mean that in terms of the EYFS Profile assessment the remainder of the 15 ELGs will be assessed in whichever language the child communicates in as these assess other aspects of their learning and development that are not specifically related to the ability to communicate in English.

This, in turn, has two implications:

1. That if a child's home language is one other than English a clear understanding of their language development will need to be obtained in order to ascertain whether there is developmental language delay which could be masked if the spoken language is not English.

2. Every effort will need to be made, within the principle and practice of observational assessment, to ensure that a true and authentic view of the child's knowledges, skills and understandings are obtained for the remaining ELG judgements, as well as the 'characteristics of effective learning' that a child would demonstrate in their home language.

To support both of these implications, the *Handbook* cites the important considerations of:

• Open and transparent communication with parents/carers in order to establish a 'two way flow of information and expertise' and clarify understandings and levels of development through the parent/carer's use of the child's home language

• Where appropriate and possible, utilising the skills, perceptions and understanding of bilingual speakers

- The importance of 'responsible pedagogy' that values the child as an individual, celebrating their culture and heritage and ensuring that the environment – and therefore the conditions for effective assessment – are optimised to enable children to demonstrate what they know and can do. (STA 2012: 9)

Lying at the heart of the revised EYFS Profile, and the single biggest 'material' change, the guidance also clarifies in detail the distinctions between the three 'best fit' bands of judgement and their relationship to the 'central core' of the statutory ELGs, with additional advice and guidance on the interpretation and implications of each in turn.

The key principles that underpin making the judgement ensure that the practitioner considers each child separately in the context of each of the 17 ELGs that will be assessed. Critically, it is made clear that the starting point is not the ELG itself but the practitioner's knowledge of the child, gleaned from observations and interactions over the year and the perspectives of other adults, particularly the parent/carer and the child themselves. Considering this information and knowledge, the practitioner will then consider the ELG statement in its entirety and then make a decision as to whether this broadly describes the child's knowledge and understanding. It is from this decision, wholly based on practitioner knowledge, that the final assessment that the EYFS Profile consists of is made.

For example, below is ELG 11: Numbers:

> Children count reliably with numbers from one to 20, place them in order and say which number is one more or one less than a given number. Using quantities and objects, they add and subtract two single-digit numbers and count on or back to find the answer. They solve problems, including doubling, halving and sharing. (STA 2012: 12)

The practitioner would approach this, armed internally with everything that they know about the child as a mathematician – how they use number, especially in the self-initiated activity, how they understand the relationship between numbers and how they utilise number operations and aspects in their everyday activity. There might be a temptation to 'separate out' each specific component and create a fragmented 'tick list' of the different parts. This is strongly discouraged by the *Handbook*:

> Practitioners must consider the entirety of each ELG and avoid splitting the descriptor into sections and ticking them off when making the decision. To create the most accurate picture of the child's overall embedded learning an holistic view of the descriptor should be taken. (STA 2012: 11)

The ELG itself is a broad description of mathematical understanding and it is this that the practitioner must relate to their knowledge and understanding of the child. There are no 'weightings' for different parts and no one aspect overrides another in importance. For example, if a child is not confident to 'count reliably with numbers from one to 20' it does not mean that the ELG in its entirety is not a broad description of the child's knowledge and understanding; if the remainder of the statement is confidently assured and ably demonstrated by the child, then this would still constitute an accurate description of the child's attainment. There is no requirement that any specific portion or percentage of the statement must be embedded in order to define this, but it will rest with the confidence of the practitioner as a 'professional decision' in how the judgement is then made, and how confident the practitioner is that this is an accurate description of the child's attainment in the specific area.

If the practitioner is not confident that the statement reflects their knowledge of the child in that ELG, then a judgement of **'emerging'** results is made. This means that the child is working below the ELG level – the expectation for the end of the EYFS. There is no specific criteria for this judgement and therefore no exemplification. A judgement of 'emerging' simply means that the child is not working securely within the ELG. This is potentially a massively broad spectrum of development and attainment that contains no differentiation within it. All children, regardless of relative attainment and development, but who are not secure within the ELG statement will be assessed in the summative EYFS Profile as 'emerging'. In practice this is potentially highly problematic. For example, the typical 'summer born boy', not yet 5 when the judgement is made, could be at a particular level of development that will flourish and emerge as the next few months in a Y1 class unfold. This is not an uncommon phenomenon, but for the purposes of the EYFS Profile, the summative assessment will be one of 'emerging'. Equally, there could be a child with profound and significant Special Educational Needs who requires continual one-to-one support. This child will equally be assessed for the summative EYFS Profile as 'emerging'. Both children will appear identical on any resulting database, even though their individual needs and developments as learners are significantly different. Therefore, the judgement of 'emerging' by itself is a particularly unhelpful and useless statement to make about a child's attainment, and will need to be supplemented with contextual clarification of the 'nature and level' of what the term 'emerging' means for each child in each case. This is acknowledged in the *Handbook* which states that:

> Where children have an outcome of emerging for an ELG within the EYFS Profile, it is likely that this will not provide full information about their

learning and development at the end of the EYFS. Additional information should be considered alongside EYFS Profile outcomes, to ensure that conversations between EYFS and Year 1 staff are meaningful, and lead to successful transition for the child. (STA 2012: 11)

It remains the case, as with the previous (EY)FSP, that a child attaining an 'emerging' level of development would still require the specific challenges of the ELGs – rather than the National Curriculum – as they transferred into Y1, as this would be more appropriate in a pedagogical and developmental sense.

When the practitioner considers what they know about the child, references the specific ELG with the appropriate exemplification and concludes that this does indeed broadly describe the child, then the judgement of **'expected'** follows. In practice, this means that the practitioner considers the child to be working securely within the ELG as defined by the statement 'A child's learning and development can be judged to be at the level expected at the end of the EYFS if the ELG description and accompanying exemplification best fit the practitioner's professional knowledge of the child' (STA 2012: 11). As stated above, this judgement is based on a professional practitioner decision based on the knowledge of the child and taking into account multiple perspectives. When making this decision, practitioners need to be confident that even if the child does not attain every single aspect of the ELG criteria the broad thrust of the statement accurately describes the child. Unlike the previous judgement of 'emerging', this criteria is specific and detailed and the EYFS Profile *Handbook* is accompanied by extensive exemplification that focuses purely on the 'pitch' and 'level of development' that children attaining the 'expected' judgement would need to attain.

The extensive exemplification that is provided alongside the *Handbook* contains thorough and comprehensive examples of the 'pitch' and level of each of the ELGs and demonstrates the nature of the 'expected judgement'. However, it is imperative that practitioners read the 'small print', as discussed above, regarding recording, documentation and evidencing their judgements. The exemplification, although an expression of content, unhelpfully appears to implicitly suggest that vast and meticulously recorded notes, narratives and photographs are required to justify the judgement. The principles of recording and the emphasis on practitioner judgement in both the statutory EYFS framework and the EYFS Profile *Handbook* make it clear that this is not the case.

If, however, on considering the child in the context of a specific ELG, the practitioner concludes that not only does the child meet all aspects of the criteria, but that they are attaining significantly beyond and above it in terms of challenge and attainment, then they must consider whether or not the judgement of **'exceeding'** should be made. The implications of this judgement would be that the child is working significantly beyond the ELG and requires specific and considered challenge as they continue into Year 1. Although there is no National Curriculum equivalent, there is an assumption that the child would already begin to attain within the current Level descriptors. However, making the judgement of 'exceeding' is more complex and requires a 'triangulation' of aspects before such an assertion is concluded. In addition to the judgement that the child is secure within all aspects of the appropriate ELG and that this inadequately describes their attainment as they have moved beyond it, the *Handbook* suggests that the following strategies are also used to consolidate the decision.

Firstly, the practitioner should familiarise themselves with the current National Curriculum Key Stage 1 Level Descriptors and attainment targets to provide a sense of whether this describes the child's attainment that is currently beyond the ELG.

Secondly, a set of descriptors is included in the *Handbook* to guide the judgement. No exemplification accompanies this and the suggestion is that this feeds into and contributes to the practitioner's overall judgement. For example, the 'exceeding' descriptor of ELG 11: Numbers, which was used previously, is as follows: 'Children estimate a number of objects and check quantities by counting up to 20. They solve practical problems that involve combining groups of 2, 5 or 10, or sharing into equal groups' (STA 2012: 12).

Finally, the practitioner is required to discuss the child, their attainment and the possible judgement of exceeding with the Y1 teacher in order to consolidate and embed the decision.

At the time of writing, this situation is further complicated by the on-going review of the National Curriculum, and a consultation is currently in effect. The results of this will inevitably impact on the nature and content of 'exceeding' judgements, which is acknowledged in the EYFS Profile Handbook: 'Arrangements for the exceeding level are interim and are subject to change once the National Curriculum review is complete' (STA 2012: 12).

A suggested format for recording the ELG judgements is included in the guidance materials, but there is no requirement that this specific format is used. Practitioners are required to make judgements for each of the

ELGs and ascribe either 'emerging', 'expected' or 'exceeding' for each.

As discussed previously, an additional and welcome requirement of the new EYFS Profile is 'a short commentary on each child's skills and abilities in relation to the three key characteristics of effective learning'. The purpose of this is to inform and enable the Y1 teacher to optimise the opportunities and possibilities for children by being aware of their specific and individual 'learning behaviours'. This commentary is in essence a 'pure' assessment, in that its specific and only possible purpose is to support the child's learning and development, no 'levelling' or 'expectation' is involved, and it culminates in a description of 'how the child learns most effectively'.

Again, there is a suggested format for practitioner to use to complete the statements for the child's characteristics as a learner. Again, there is no requirement to use this and the separation between the three aspects is unhelpful. Considering the overlaps within the nature and content of these three characteristics, practitioners may consider dispensing with the lines that separate them, simply providing a narrative of a few sentences that best describe the child as a learner, and highlighting the particular attributes and behaviours that the receiving Y1 teacher will need to be aware of in order to optimise learning opportunities and outcomes.

As with previous versions of the EYFS Profile, a system of moderating the ultimately subjective judgements that practitioners make will be in place in order to ensure that there is a national consistency and confidence in the data – information – that results from it.

A consistent national database arising from these judgements has a far greater importance than the strategic and political uses to which it is and will be applied. We will discuss these in more detail later. The accuracy and consistency of this data matters because it enshrines and protects key aspects of effective, and hard fought for, Early Years pedagogy and provision. The importance of observing children in self-initiated activity, of including all aspects of learning and development, of identifying the how, the learning behaviours through the 'characteristics of effective learning', and the importance of including multiple perspectives of knowledge and the expertise and knowledge of the practitioner – recorded or not – are vital aspects of developing approaches that focus on the reality of children's learning and development and the very principles of purpose and aspiration that assessment supports. By contributing to a consistent database in which there is 'statistical confidence' practitioners are ensuring that key tenets of pedagogy are enshrined and that any accountability – internal or external – will at the very least have a reasonable and appropriate starting point.

Therefore, the moderation approach, overseen by and the responsibility of the Local Authority, is an important mechanism in establishing confidence in the process and the outcomes. The documentation makes it clear that the purpose of moderation is to:

- secure the consistency and accuracy of judgements made by different practitioners;
- reassure practitioners that their judgements are accurate, valid and consistent with national standards
- assure moderators that an acceptable level of accuracy and validity has been achieved for assessments recorded and reported by the settings for which they have responsibility. (STA 2012: 31)

Local Authority appointed moderators will then scrutinise practitioner judgements to ensure that the decisions made are consistent with the exemplification and the national understanding of what constitutes an outcome of 'emerging', 'expected' or exceeding'. These will take place through 'moderation meetings', evidence trialling of practitioners' information or moderation visits, when the moderator scrutinises the decisions and judgements made in situ. Generally, the focus of this will be identified Prime and Specific ELG outcomes, and Local Authorities will inform practitioners of their own strategic decisions on this. It is neither the role of the moderator nor the purpose of the moderation process to assess the practitioner's knowledge and understanding of the child, but how this knowledge relates to the criteria of the ELGs and how the final judgement is made. The mechanism for this is described as: 'Moderation focuses on a professional dialogue between moderators and practitioners in order to ensure that practitioner judgements are consistent with the national exemplification of standards, and that the assessment of attainment is reliable, accurate and secure' (STA 2012: 31).

This dialogue is expressed through the practitioner knowledge and understanding and rests heavily on the principles of the EYFS profile explored in depth earlier in this chapter. It is practitioner knowledge that provides the information for the judgement and therefore it is the same practitioner knowledge that is the subject of moderation. It is also worth revisiting the statement on 'evidencing judgements for the purpose of moderation':

Practitioners and EYFS Profile moderators should be aware that the definition of evidence is any material, knowledge of the child, anecdotal incident or result of observation or information from additional sources that supports the overall picture of a child's development. There is no requirement that it should be formally recorded or documented; the extent to which the practitioner chooses to record information will depend on individual preference. Paperwork should be kept to the minimum that practitioners require to illustrate, support and recall their knowledge of the child's attainment. (STA 2012: 12)

Practitioners will be required to report the outcomes of the EYFS Profile summative assessment and, in addition to submitting the data, when requested, to the Local Authority, will need to make the more usable information available. A copy of the outcomes and the narrative of the 'characteristics of effective learning' will form part of the transition to Y1 and inform the receiving teacher of the information it contains. They will then use this to ensure that their provision and pedagogy will be shaped appropriately around the incoming cohort to ensure that needs are met, challenges are set and the individuality of each learner is acknowledged. Parents/carers will also be informed of the specific outcomes through the end of year report which is described as needing to be concise, informative and specific to the child. In addition to this a consultation with the parent/carer in which this is discussed will also need to take place. Practitioners and settings may need to take a view on which would be the most appropriate platform for discussion of the 'raw scores' of the EYFS Profile. Although there is a requirement that this is shared explicitly with parents, an interpretation of whether this is best in a written report or a consultation is a decision for practitioners. However, there is a specific requirement that the report to parents must include a 'written summary of their child's attainment using the 17 ELGs and a narrative on how a child demonstrates the three characteristics of effective learning' (STA 2012: 7).

The documentation notes that 'The *primary purpose* of the EYFS Profile is to provide a reliable, valid and accurate assessment of individual children at the end of the EYFS'. The uses of this data, for parents/carers, Reception practitioners and Year 1 teachers is clearly within the principles of the uses of information, answering Mary Jane Drummond's question 'how can we put this information to good use?'. There are clear reasons for EYFS practitioners to use the attainment of ELGs and the nature of the 'Characteristics of effective learning' to reflect on, review and develop their provision, in addition to its more 'clinical' use as a means for both internal and external accountability. Equally, as already discussed, Year 1 teachers will be able to assimilate and process the information that this summative assessment provides to consider how best to support and challenge the children as they transfer from the EYFS. For example, how will children assessed as 'emerging' be supported? How will children assessed as 'exceeding' be challenged? How will the individual traits identified in the accompanying narrative guide and shape interactions and expectations of the child? How will this be used to optimise the conditions and contexts for continued learning and development? (Drummond 1993).

However, there is also an acknowledgement that the *'secondary purpose* of the assessment is to provide an accurate national data set relating to levels of child development at the end of the EYFS which can be used to monitor changes in levels of children's development/school readiness nationally and locally' (Drummond 1993). A definition of a 'good level of development' has also been published in order to provide the broad 'expectation' against which such monitoring can take place. This will now consist of an attainment of at least 'expected' in all the Prime Areas of Learning and Development – Personal Social and Emotional Development, Communication and Language and Physical Development – in addition to the two specific areas of Mathematics and Literacy.

The 'external' use of data is always a vexed issue as the use itself can often unintentionally compromise the accuracy and honesty of the information and therefore undermine its key purpose – to accurately describe learners in order to support their on-going development. Needless to say, much anxiety has persisted around how 'progress and development' is described – or even measured – within the EYFS itself. There is a clear statement that the EYSF Profile is not the mechanism for this: 'The EYFS Profile is not intended to be used for on-going assessment or for entry level assessment for Early Years settings or Reception classes' (STA 2012: 5) and the only time the language of the 3 Es should be used is at the end of the EYFS at the point of transfer to Year 1. The suggestion for this is the revised 'Development Matters'/Early Years Outcomes statements in its non-statutory form in which it is stated that 'Early Years providers will find these useful in helping them to make judgements about the on-going monitoring and assessment of children, prior to undertaking the EYFS profile' (STA 2012: 5). But, as has already been discussed, this approach is riven with problems, inconsistencies and non sequiturs, and the statements in the column of the 'unique child' which purport to describe what children do are in no way a definitive view or description of child development. Fortunately, the non-statutory status of the documents enables practitioners to interpret, discard, embellish, select and modify the statements to create something that is more meaningful and sensible to them. In this context the overlapping age-related bands do provide a useful framework and could be then used by EYFS practitioners to describe the development and journeys that children are making in the setting. Although the OFSTED approach to measuring progress in the EYFS focuses on the developments children make in terms of the 'age-related bands of expectation' it is important to consider that this is in itself a 'starting point' for understanding development and progress rather than a definitive calculation. Within children's eventual progression through these bands lies an extensive and rich plethora of stores, incidents, thought trajectories, involvement, engagement and other critical significances and 'signifiers' that constitute effective and meaningful learning and development. Practitioners will need to be clear, drawing on OFSTED's own guidance that 'Schools should have clear systems to:

- make an assessment of children's starting points (baseline)

- plan next steps that challenge children sufficiently

- track the progress of individuals, groups of children and cohorts across the Early Years Foundation Stage and into Key Stage 1

- identify how much progress is made by individuals as well as groups of children and the cohort' (OFSTED 2013)

and that 'there is no requirement for schools to be generating hundreds of assessments for every child. They must develop an approach that meets the needs of their children, informs teaching and demonstrates children's progress from their starting points. Inspectors should sample from the school's system' (OFSTED 2013).

Below are examples of completed EYFS Profiles for four children; the contextual information for each is as follows:

Child A: Child attaining the 'expected' level of development with one aspect that is 'exceeding'

Child B: Child attaining within the 'expected' level of development

Child C: Summer-born boy, attaining at the 'emerging' level of development

Child D: Child speaking English as an Additional Language (EAL)

Child E: Child speaking English as an Additional Language (EAL)

Child A.

Area of learning		Aspect	Emerging	Expected	Exceeding
Communication and language	ELG 01	Listening and attention		✓	
	ELG 02	Understanding		✓	
	ELG 03	Speaking		✓	
Physical development	ELG 04	Moving and handling		✓	
	ELG 05	Health and self-care		✓	
Personal, social and emotional development	ELG 06	Self-confidence and self-awareness			✓
	ELG 07	Managing feelings and behaviour		✓	
	ELG 08	Making relationships		✓	
Literacy	ELG 09	Reading		✓	
	ELG 10	Writing		✓	
Mathematics	ELG 11	Numbers		✓	
	ELG 12	Shapes, space and measures		✓	
Understanding the world	ELG 13	People and communities		✓	
	ELG 14	The world		✓	
	ELG 15	Technology		✓	
Expressive arts and design	ELG 16	Exploring and using media and materials		✓	
	ELG 17	Being imaginative		✓	

Annex 1: EYFS Profile

Name...Child...A......   Age in months......5yr 5months

Characteristics of effective learning	How (name of child) learns
By playing and exploring: • finding out and exploring • using what they know in their play • being willing to have a go	A___ now fully involves herself in play and challenges that she sets herself. At the beginning of the year she was watchful of the other children and would occasionally wipe her "leaky eyes". In April she observed another child pedaling the "wobbly 2 wheeler bike" and attempted it once
Through active learning: • being involved and concentrating • keeping on trying • enjoying achieving what they set out to do	herself. Yesterday she told the teacher she was going to learn how to do the bike. She tried over and over again. Today she proudly asked lots of different teachers to watch her cycle without falling. A___ loves to write and she
By creating and thinking critically • having their own ideas • using what they already know to learn new things • choosing ways to do things and finding new ways	uses her competence to build relationships and creatively makes up games. Yesterday she went round asking "Who wants to go swimming?" using a clipboard and writing children's names, if they did want to swim.

52 2013 Early Years Foundation Stage Profile Handbook

Child B

Area of learning		Aspect	Emerging	Expected	Exceeding
Communication and language	ELG 01	Listening and attention		✓	
	ELG 02	Understanding		✓	
	ELG 03	Speaking		✓	
Physical development	ELG 04	Moving and handling		✓	
	ELG 05	Health and self-care		✓	
Personal, social and emotional development	ELG 06	Self-confidence and self-awareness		✓	
	ELG 07	Managing feelings and behaviour		✓	
	ELG 08	Making relationships		✓	
Literacy	ELG 09	Reading		✓	
	ELG 10	Writing		✓	
Mathematics	ELG 11	Numbers		✓	
	ELG 12	Shapes, space and measures		✓	
Understanding the world	ELG 13	People and communities		✓	
	ELG 14	The world		✓	
	ELG 15	Technology		✓	
Expressive arts and design	ELG 16	Exploring and using media and materials	✓		
	ELG 17	Being imaginative	✓		

Annex 1: EYFS Profile

Name...*Child B*...

Age in months...*5 years 4 months*...

Characteristics of effective learning	How (name of child) learns
By playing and exploring: • finding out and exploring • using what they know in their play • being willing to have a go	B— likes to talk and quite often in a matter-of-fact way. "This is boring" he said towards the end of a phonics session. He has a strong sense of self, is decisive and likes to ask questions. He most enjoys learning outside with the water, bikes and hollow blocks. He will stay developing an imaginative game for a full session
Through active learning: • being involved and concentrating • keeping on trying • enjoying achieving what they set out to do	and return to it over and over again. He will often get "filfthy" which he jokes about when his mum picks him up. He enjoys achieving and uses his new skills such as when he wrote a name label to protect an elaborate mobilo model he had made.
By creating and thinking critically • having their own ideas • using what they already know to learn new things • choosing ways to do things and finding new ways	C—'s imagination is also apparent in his drawings as he regularly stories through pictures, such as "here's a castle... it's magic door..... then the dragon comes...." Today he drew a picture of himself, smiling and proudly said "it's me, because I'm always happy!"

52 2013 Early Years Foundation Stage Profile Handbook

Child C

Area of learning		Aspect	Emerging	Expected	Exceeding
Communication and language	ELG 01	Listening and attention	✓		
	ELG 02	Understanding	✓		
	ELG 03	Speaking	✓		
Physical development	ELG 04	Moving and handling		✓	
	ELG 05	Health and self-care	✓		
Personal, social and emotional development	ELG 06	Self-confidence and self-awareness		✓	
	ELG 07	Managing feelings and behaviour		✓	
	ELG 08	Making relationships		✓	
Literacy	ELG 09	Reading	✓		
	ELG 10	Writing	✓		
Mathematics	ELG 11	Numbers	✓		
	ELG 12	Shapes, space and measures	✓		
Understanding the world	ELG 13	People and communities	✓		
	ELG 14	The world		✓	
	ELG 15	Technology		✓	
Expressive arts and design	ELG 16	Exploring and using media and materials		✓	
	ELG 17	Being imaginative		✓	

Annex 1: EYFS Profile

Name... Child   C .....

Age in months...... 4 years 11 months

Characteristics of effective learning	How (name of child) learns
By playing and exploring: • finding out and exploring • using what they know in their play • being willing to have a go	C— is incredibly imaginative. Following a trip he made a farm with the birds and animals then combined the weather focus and a "thunderstorm" hit and "washed the animals away". He has an equally imaginative close friend; they role play Batman adventures, day after day, taking turns each day to be Batman.
Through active learning: • being involved and concentrating • keeping on trying • enjoying achieving what they set out to do	C— gets involves + concentrates well within his own activities. He will occasionally join adult-directed tasks yet will stop if it is too difficult, such as when his fingers couldn't twist the number spinner to make it work or he will look dreamy if a large group session does not interest him.
By creating and thinking critically • having their own ideas • using what they already know to learn new things • choosing ways to do things and finding new ways	The art area interests C— He regularly explores mixing powder paint ...."I've made orange." Recently he made a model DS device, sticking buttons and a hole to insert cartridges. At the end of the day he put it in his home tray but carried on with it the next morning.

52 2013 Early Years Foundation Stage Profile Handbook

Child D

Area of learning		Aspect	Emerging	Expected	Exceeding
Communication and language	ELG 01	Listening and attention	✓		
	ELG 02	Understanding	✓		
	ELG 03	Speaking		✓*	
Physical development	ELG 04	Moving and handling	✓		
	ELG 05	Health and self-care		✓	
Personal, social and emotional development	ELG 06	Self-confidence and self-awareness	✓		
	ELG 07	Managing feelings and behaviour		✓	
	ELG 08	Making relationships		✓	
Literacy	ELG 09	Reading		✓	
	ELG 10	Writing	~~✓~~	✓	
Mathematics	ELG 11	Numbers	✓		
	ELG 12	Shapes, space and measures	✓		
Understanding the world	ELG 13	People and communities	✓		
	ELG 14	The world	✓		
	ELG 15	Technology		✓	
Expressive arts and design	ELG 16	Exploring and using media and materials		✓	
	ELG 17	Being imaginative		✓	

* Extensively moderated. On cusp of 'emerging' into 'expected'.

Annex 1: EYFS Profile

Name...... Child D ......

Age in months...... 4 years 10 months

Characteristics of effective learning	How (name of child) learns
By playing and exploring: • finding out and exploring • using what they know in their play • being willing to have a go	When D—— started school in April she played with children in Arabic As her English developed she started to communicate with more children + practitioners. D—— is a prolific writer and regularly wants to take writing area resources home. She took
Through active learning: • being involved and concentrating • keeping on trying • enjoying achieving what they set out to do	some paper and clips one day and reappeared the next day with a beautiful book. She made drawings of her family and lists their names. Recently she is becoming more imaginative in her drawings when she draws monsters. They are becoming increasingly
By creating and thinking critically • having their own ideas • using what they already know to learn new things • choosing ways to do things and finding new ways	intricate and detailed. D—— is incredibly enthusiastic "I love coming to school!" "I want a go!" to be one of the 5 currant buns or "let me in" to see the newly hatched chicks. D—— enjoy exploring and the texture of damp sand. She insists she has a new

book to take home everyday and asks for a new phonics flashcard when she has learnt all the ones she has already taken home.

52 2013 Early Years Foundation Stage Profile Handbook

Child E

Area of learning		Aspect	Emerging	Expected	Exceeding
Communication and language	ELG 01	Listening and attention		✓	
	ELG 02	Understanding		✓	
	ELG 03	Speaking	✓		
Physical development	ELG 04	Moving and handling		✓	
	ELG 05	Health and self-care	✓		
Personal, social and emotional development	ELG 06	Self-confidence and self-awareness		✓	
	ELG 07	Managing feelings and behaviour		✓	
	ELG 08	Making relationships		✓	
Literacy	ELG 09	Reading		✓	
	ELG 10	Writing	✓		
Mathematics	ELG 11	Numbers	✓		
	ELG 12	Shapes, space and measures	✓		
Understanding the world	ELG 13	People and communities	✓		
	ELG 14	The world		✓	
	ELG 15	Technology	✓		
Expressive arts and design	ELG 16	Exploring and using media and materials		✓	
	ELG 17	Being imaginative		✓	

Further reading 📖

Dubiel, J. (2013) 'Tiaras may be optional – the truth isn't: the Early Years Foundation Stage Profile and accurate assessment', in S. Featherstone (ed.) *Supporting Child-initiated Learning: Like Bees not Butterflies.* London: Featherstone.

Standards and Testing Agency (2013) *Early Years Foundation Stage Profile Handbook.* DfE.

Bibliography

Abbott, L. and Moylett, H. (eds) (1999) *Early Education Transformed*. London: Falmer Press.

Abbott, L. and Nutbrown, C. (2001) *Experiencing Reggio Emilia: Implications for Pre-school Provision*. Maidenhead: Open University Press.

Allen, G. (2011) *Early Intervention: The Next Steps*. HM Government.

Anning, A. and Edwards, A. (eds) (2003) *Promoting Children's Learning from Birth to Five: Developing the New Early Years Professional*. Maidenhead: Open University Press.

Assessment Reform Group (2002) *Assessment for Learning – 10 Principles*. Available at: http://www.assessmentreformgroup.files.wordpress.com/2012/01/10principles_english.pdf

Bancroft, S. et al. (2008) *Researching Children: Researching the World: 5x5x5 = Creativity*. Stoke on Trent: Trentham Books.

Barber, J. and Paul-Smith, S. (2012) *Early Years Observation and Planning in Practice: Your Guide to Best Practice and Use of Different Methods for Planning and Observation in the EYFS*. London: Practical Pre-School Books.

Best, B. (2012) 'Values and effective teaching', published in *Teaching Expertise*. Available at: http://www.teachingexpertise.com/articles/values-effective-teaching-466

Blenkin, G. (1992) 'Progression, observation and assessment in early education: the context', in G.M. Blenkin et al., *Assessment in Early Childhood Education*. London: Paul Chapman.

Blenkin, G. and Kelly, A.V. (eds) (1992) *Assessment in Early Childhood Education*. London: Paul Chapman.

Bredekamp, S. and Copple, C. (1997) *Developmentally Appropriate Practice*. Washington, DC: National Association for the Education of Young Children.

Broadfoot, S. (1996) 'Assessment and learning: power or partnership?', in H. Goldstein and T. Lewis (eds) *Assessment: Problems, Developments and Statistical Issues*. Chichester: John Wiley.

Brown, S. (2003) *Celebrating Childhood: Keynote Address to the 13th Annual Conference of the European Early Childhood Education Research Association, Quality in Early Education: Possible Childhoods – Relationships and Choices*, University of Strathclyde, Glasgow.

Bruce, T. (1989) *Early Childhood Education*. London: Hodder Education.

Bruce, T. (1999) 'In praise of inspired and inspiring teachers', in L. Abbott and H. Moylett (eds) *Early Education Transformed*. London: Falmer Press.

Bruner, J. (1996) *The Culture of Education*. Cambridge, MA: Harvard University Press.

Carr, M. (2001) *Assessment in Early Childhood Settings*. London: Paul Chapman.

Carr, M. and Lee, W. (2012) *Learning Stories: Constructing Learner Identities in Early Education*. London: SAGE.

Clare, A. (2012) *Creating a Learning Environment for Babies and Toddlers*. London: SAGE.

Clarke, S. (2001) *Unlocking Formative Assessment: Practical Strategies for Enhancing Pupils Learning in the Primary Classroom*. London: Hodder Education.

Claxton, G. (2004) 'Learning is learnable (and we ought to teach it)', in *The National Commission for Education Report – Ten Years On*, edited by Sir John Cassell.

Cohen, A. and Cohen, L. (1988) *Early Education – The School Years: A Source Book for Teachers*. London: Paul Chapman.

DCSF (2008) *The Early Years Foundation Stage: Setting the Standards for Learning, Development and Care for Children from Birth to Five*. DCSF.

Department for Education (DfE) (2012) *The Statutory Framework for the Early Years Foundation Stage*. Cheshire: DfE.

Department for Education (DfE) (2013) *Early Years Outcomes*. Cheshire: DfE.

Department for Education/Department of Health (2011) *Supporting Families in the Foundation Years*. Cheshire; London: DfE.

Department for Education and Skills (2007) *Creating the Picture*. London: DfES.

Dowling, M. (1992) *Education 3–5: A Teacher's Handbook*. London: Paul Chapman.

Drummond, M.J. (1993) *Learning to See: Assessment through Observation*. York, ME: Stenhouse.

Drummond, M.J. (2008) 'Assessment and values: a close and necessary relationship', in S. Swaffield (ed.) *Unlocking Assessment*. London: David Fulton.

Dubiel, J. (2013) 'Tiaras may be optional – the truth isn't: the Early Years Foundation Stage Profile and accurate assessment', in S. Featherstone (ed.) *Supporting Child-initiated Learning: Like Bees not Butterflies*. London: Featherstone.

Duckett, R. and Drummond, M.J. (2009) *Adventuring in Early Childhood Education*. Newcastle upon Tyne: Sightlines Initiative.

Dudley, P. and Swaffield, S. (2008) 'Understanding and using assessment data', in S. Swaffield (ed.) *Unlocking Assessment*. London: David Fulton.

Dweck, C. (2006) *Mindset: The New Psychology of Success*. London: Random House.

Dweck, C. (2012) *Mindset: How You Can Fulfil your Potential*. New York: Ballantine Books.

Dworkin, A. (1982) *Our Blood: Prophesies and Discourses on Sexual Politics*. London: The Women's Press.

Earl, L. and Katz, L. (2008) 'Getting to the core of learning', in S. Swaffield (ed.) *Unlocking Assessments*. London: David Fulton.

Early Education (2012) *Development Matters in the Early Years Foundation Stage*. London: Early Education.

Edwards, C., Gandini, L. and Forman, G. (1998) *The Hundred Languages of Children: the Reggio Emilia Approach. Advanced Reflections*. New York: Ablex.

Eliot, L. (2001) *Early Intelligence: How the Brain and Mind Develop in the First Five Years of Life*. London: Penguin.

Field, F. (2010) *The Foundation Years: Preventing Poor Children Becoming Poor Adults*. London: HM Government.

Fisher, J. (2008) *Starting from the Child: Teaching and Learning from 4–8*. Maidenhead: Open University Press.

Flanagan, C. (2004) *Applying Psychology to Early Childhood Development*. London: Hodder Education.

Glazzard, J., Chadwick, D., Webster, A. and Percival, J. (2010) *Assessment for Learning in the Early Years Foundation Stage*. London: SAGE.

Gooch, K. (2010) *Towards Excellence in Early Years Education: Exploring Narratives of Experience*. London: Routledge.

Gopnik et al. (2001) *How Babies Think*. London: Pheonix.

Hargreaves, A. (1989) *Curriculum and Assessment Reform*. Maidenhead: Open University Press.

Hobcraft, J. and Kierman, K. (2010) *Predicative Factors from Age 3 and Infancy for Poor Child Outcomes at Age 5 Relating to Children's Development, Behaviour and Health: Evidence from the Millennium Cohort Study*. University of York.

Hohmann, M., Weikart, D., and Epstein, A.S. (2008) *Educating Young Children*, 3rd edn. Ypsilanti, MI: HighScope Press.

Hurst, K. and Lally, M. (1992) 'Assessment and the nursery curriculum', in G.M. Blenkin and A.V. Kelly (eds) *Assessment in Early Childhood Education*. London: Paul Chapman.

Hurst, K. and Nutbrown, C. (2005) *Perspectives on Early Childhood Education: Contemporary Research*. Stoke on Trent: Trentham Books.

Hutchin, V. (1996) *Tracking Significant Achievement in the Early Years*. London: Hodder Education.

Hutchin, V. (1999) *Right from the Start: Effective Planning and Assessment in the Early Years*. London: Hodder Education.

Hutchin, V. (2003) *Observing and Assessing for the Foundation Stage Profile*. London: Hodder Education.

Kamen, T. (2013) *Observation and Assessment for the EYFS*. London: Hodder Education.

Katz, L. (2008) *Current Perspectives on the Early Childhood Curriculum*, address to the Inaugural Conference for the OpenEYE campaign.

Katz, L. and Katz, S.J. (2009) *Intellectual Emergencies: Some Reflections on Mothering and Teaching*. KPress.

Kelly, V. (1992) 'Concepts of assessment: an overview', in G.M. Blenkin and A.V. Kelly (eds) *Assessment in Early Childhood Education*. London: Paul Chapman.

Korzybski, A. (1931) 'Science and sanity', paper delivered to American Association for the Advancement of Science.

Laevers, F. and Declercq, B. (eds) (2012) *A Process-Orientated Monitoring System for the Early Years (POMS)*. CEGO.

Lally, M. (1991) *The Nursery Teacher in Action*. London: Paul Chapman.

Lally, M. and Hurst, K. (1992) 'Assessment in Nursery Education: a review of approaches', in G.M. Blenkin and A.V. Kelly (eds) *Assessment in Early Childhood Education*. London: Paul Chapman.

Lindon, J. (2012) *Reflective Practice and Early Years Professionalism: Linking Theory and Practice (LTP)*. London: Hodder.

Lindon, J. (2012) *What Does It Mean to be Two?* London: Practical Pre-School Books.

Lloyd-Yero, J. (2010) 'Teaching in mind: how teacher thinking shapes education', published in *Teaching Expertise* (2012). Available at: http://www.teachingexpertise.com/articles/values-effective-teaching-466

Luff, P. (2013) 'Observations: recording and analysis in the Early Years Foundation Stage', in I. Palaiologou (ed.) *The Early Years Foundation Stage*, 2nd edn. London: SAGE.

Marcon, R. (2002) 'Moving up the grades: relationship between preschool model and later school success'. *Early Childhood Research and Practice*, 4(1). http://www.ecrp.uiuc.edu/v4n1/marcon.html

Marsden, L. and Woodbridge, J. (2005) *Looking Closely at Learning and Teaching … A Journey of Development*. Huddersfield: Early Excellence.

Miller, L. (2004) *Supporting Children's Learning in the Early Years*. London: David Fulton/Open University Press.

Moyles, J. (2002) *The Excellence of Play*. Maidenhead: Open University Press.

National Assessment Agency (NAA) (2007) *Supplementary Guidance for Completing the Foundation Stage Profile*. NAA.

National Children's Bureau (NCB) (2012) *A Know How Guide: The EYFS Progress Check at Age Two*. DfE.

Nutbrown, C. (2001) *Threads of Thinking: Young Children Learning and the Role of Education*. London: Paul Chapman.

Nutbrown, C. and Carter, C. (2012) 'The tools of assessment: watching and learning', in G. Pugh and B. Duffy *Contemporary Issues in the Early Years*. London: SAGE.

OFSTED (2013) *Subsidiary guidance; Supporting the inspection of maintained schools and academies*, version3.

Olson, D.R. and Bruner, J.S. (1996) 'Folk psychology and folk pedagogy', in D.R. Olson and N. Torrence (eds) *The Handbook of Education and Human Development: New Models of Teaching, Learning and Schooling*. London: Blackwell.

Penn, H. (2005) *Understanding Early Childhood: Issues and Controversies*. Maidenhead: Open University Press.

Peters, R. (1966) *Ethics and Education*. George Allen and Unwin Ltd.

Postman, N. (1982) *The Disappearance of Childhood*. New York: Vintage.

Qualifications and Curriculum Authority (QCA) (2000) *Curriculum Guidance for the Foundation Stage*. Carrickfergus: QCA.

Qualifications and Curriculum Authority (QCA) (2003) *The Foundation Stage Profile Handbook*. Carrickfergus: QCA.

Qualifications and Curriculum Authority (QCA) (2008) *Early Years Foundation Stage Profile Handbook*. Carrickfergus: QCA.

Riley, J. (2003) *Learning in the Early Years: A Guide for Teachers of Children 3–7*. London: Paul Chapman.

Rogers, S. et al. (2011) *Rethinking Play and Pedagogy in Early Childhood Education*. Abingdon: Routledge.

Rose, J. and Rogers, S. (2012) *The Role of the Adult in Early Years Settings*. Maidenhead: McGrawHill.

Säljö, R. (1979) 'Learning in the learner's perspective 1: some commonplace misconceptions', *Reports from the Institute of Education*, University of Gothenburg, 76. Quoted in J.S. Atherton (2011) *Learning and Teaching: Deep and Surface Learning* [On-line: UK] Available at: http://www.learningandteaching.info/learning/deepsurf.htm (accessed 25 May 2013).

School Curriculum and Assessment Authority (SCAA) (1996) *The Desirable Outcomes for Children's Learning*. SCAA.

School Curriculum and Assessment Authority (SCAA) (1997) *The National Framework for Baseline Assessment*. SCAA.

Schweinhart, L., Montie, J., Xiang, Z., Barnett, W.S., Belfield, C.R. and Nores, M. (2005) *Lifetime Effects: The HighScope Perry Preschool Study Through Age 40*. Ypsilanti, MI: HighScope Press.

Shore, R. (1997) *Rethinking the Brain: New Insights into Early Development*. New York: Families and Work Institute.

Siraj-Blatchford, I. (2008) 'Understanding the relationship between curriculum, pedagogy and progression in Learning in Early Childhood', *Hong Kong Journal of Early Childhood*. 7(2): 6–13.

Siraj-Blatchford, I. (2009) 'Quality teaching in the early years', in A. Anning, J. Cullen and M. Fleer (eds) Early Childhood Education: Society and culture, p. 147.

Standards and Testing Agency (STA) (2012) *Early Years Foundation Stage Profile Handbook*. DfE.

Stewart, N. (2011) *How Children Learn: The Characteristics of Effective Early Learning*. London: Early Education.

Stipek, D., Feiler, R., Daniels, D. and Milburn, S. (1995) 'Effects of different instructional approaches on young children's achievement and motivation', *Child Development*, 66(1): 209–23. EJ 501 879.

Surestart (2003) *Birth to Three Matters: A Framework to Support Children in their Earliest Years*. Surestart.

Swaffield, S. (ed.) (2008) *Unlocking Assessment: Understanding for Reflection and Application*. London: David Fulton.

Sylva, K., Melhuish, E., Sammons, P., Siraj-Blatchford, I. and Taggart, B. (2010) *Early Childhood Matters: Evidence from the Effective Pre-school and Primary Education Project (EPPE)*. Abingdon: Routledge.

Tickell, C. (2011) *The Early Years: Foundations for Life, Health and Learning: An Independent Report on the Early Years Foundation Stage to Her Majesty's Government*. Cheshire: DfE.

Vygotsky, L. (1978) *Mind in Society: The Development of Higher Psychological Processes*. Cambridge, MA: Harvard University Press.

Whitebread, D. (2012) *Developmental Psychology and Early Childhood Education*. London: SAGE.

Index